by Jean-François Revel

t Marx or Jesus

alitarian Temptation

mocracies Perish

t from Truth:
of Deceit in the Age of Information

and the Philosopher:
d Son Discuss the Meaning of Life

gainst Itself:
f the Democratic Impulse

ANTI-AMERI

ANTI-AMERICANISM
JEAN-FRANÇOIS REVEL

Translated from the French by Diarmid Cammell

ENCOUNTER BOOKS
SAN FRANCISCO

First English language edition published in 2003 by Encounter Books, an activity of Encounter for Culture and Education, Inc., a nonprofit tax exempt corporation. Copyright © 2003 by Encounter Books.

Originally published in France as *L'obsession anti-américaine: Son fonctionnement, ses causes, ses inconséquences* in 2000 by Plon.

Encounter Books website address: www.encounterbooks.com
Manufactured in the United States and printed on acid-free paper.

The paper used in this publication meets the minimum requirements of ANSI/NISO Z39.48-1992 (R 1997) (*Permanence of Paper*).

Library of Congress Cataloging-in-Publication Data

Revel, Jean-François.
    [Obsession anti-américaine. English] Anti-Americanism / Jean-François Revel.
    p.   cm.
    Includes bibliographical references.
    ISBN 1-893554-85-6 (alk. paper)
    1. Anti-Americanism.   2. United States—Foreign relations—1945–1989.
    3. United States—Foreign relations—1989– .   I. Title.
    E840 .R4313 2003
    303.48'273—dc22

                                                                2003061557

10   9   8   7   6   5   4   3   2

To Olivier Orban, instigator,
in gratitude and friendship

Contents

Introduction

IN 2000, MY FRIEND AND PUBLISHER Olivier Orban suggested that I embark on a sequel to a book, *Without Marx or Jesus,* that I wrote thirty years ago. His idea was that, like its predecessor, it should deal substantially with the United States, with attitudes towards the United States, and with how those attitudes have evolved since 1970.

At the time, the idea didn't seem too foolhardy. Mainly between 1970 and 1990, and after that rather less, I had traveled frequently in the United States, sometimes making quite a lengthy stay. From inside the country as well as outside, I had been an attentive watcher of the United States' ever-expanding role in world affairs after the disappearance of the Soviet Union and during the gradual erosion of Chinese Communism. And I had remained fairly *au courant* with the literature and reportage on developments within the United States and the huge geopolitical changes that followed her accession to the rank of "sole global superpower."

Yet I soon came to question my initial reaction and reined in my enthusiasm for a task that Olivier's optimism had lured me into. As my new book progressed—or rather, barely progressed—the undertaking loomed ever more difficult and complex. It became harder and harder to cut a path "through the thorns and brambles of dialectic" (in Taine's phrase)—that is, to clear a way through the thickets that stand between observation and synthesis.

Before explaining why this was so, I must ask for the reader's patience while I describe the circumstances that impelled me in 1970 to write *Without Marx or Jesus.* It is a book you could describe, for want of a better word, as accidental. In 1969, *Time* magazine got the idea of bringing out a French edition. There was one problem with this plan: how to

1

develop a French equivalent of the terse, concise, almost telegraphic writing style of *Time,* with its characteristic short phrases and complete absence of waffle and padding. Ever since the weekly's founding in the 1920s, this style has been emulated by journalists everywhere; uniting brevity and clarity, it is far easier to do in English than in French and the other Latinate languages.

I was good friends with *Time* magazine's Paris bureau chief and permanent staff, both as a colleague and because *Time* was then the principal shareholder of the big publishing house of Robert Laffont, for whom I was a literary advisor. Apparently they considered my articles in *L'Express* compatible with their concept of economical journalism, since they suggested to their parent organization that I might like to experiment with translating *Time*'s American English into French. The idea was that I would spend a few weeks in New York City attempting to reproduce a few issues of the magazine in the approved style. If they judged my efforts convincing, *Time* would go ahead with their Paris project.

Things moved quickly. My prospective employers had reserved a room for me in a New York hotel; I had my visa and my airline ticket. But then, belatedly, it suddenly dawned on me and began to nag at my conscience that a French *Time* would inevitably become a competitor of *L'Express,* with which I had contractual obligations as well as long-term personal friendships. So it was out of the question that I accept the Americans' offer without first getting permission from the managing editor, Jean-Jacques Servan-Schreiber—author, incidentally, of *Le Défi américain* ("The American Challenge"). My concerns were well founded, since he immediately voiced his opposition to my getting involved in the project.

Sheepishly, I went straightaway to see Curtis Prendergast, *Time*'s Paris bureau chief, to offer my apologies: my behavior had been thoughtless, and I had let him down. Prendergast, however nonplussed he might reasonably have felt, is an affable man and he didn't reproach me in the least.

But soon after—again, a delayed reaction—I had a brainstorm: I would make the trip to the United States anyway. Since *L'Express* had insisted that I drop the project, I felt the magazine owed me something in return. So I decided to present my brilliant idea to the literary editor, Françoise Giroud: over lunch at Taillevent's, I suggested that an all-expenses-paid trip to the U.S.A. would, from my point of view, be entirely adequate compensation for my frustrated *Time* ambitions. My colleague barely blinked; back in her office at *L'Express* that afternoon, she gave instructions for airline tickets and an advance on expenses.

From 1953 to 1969, living in Italy and then in France, I had watched and formed my opinion about the United States through the filter of the European press, which means that my judgment was unfavorable. Europeans at that time saw America as the land of McCarthyism and the execution of the Rosenbergs (who were innocent, we believed), of racism and the Korean War and a stranglehold on Europe itself—the "American occupation of France," as Simone de Beauvoir and the Communists used to say. And then Vietnam became the principal reason to hate America.

Since the end of the Cold War—with the collapse of the Soviet Union, the liberation of Eastern Europe, and the realignment of a polarized world—it is often said that today's anti-Americanism derives from the fact that the United States is now the "hyperpower," a term made fashionable by Hubert Védrine, a French minister of foreign affairs. This interpretation assumes that American hegemony was previously easier to justify, first because it dominated fewer nations and second because it answered to the need to protect against Soviet imperialism. But this doesn't reflect reality: anti-Americanism was almost as virulent during the period of threatening totalitarianism as it has been after that threat disappeared (in its Soviet version, at least).

Within some democratic countries, a subset of the population, some political parties and the majority of intellectuals, were prone to adhere to Communism, or at least support similar ideas. For this crowd, anti-Americanism was rational, since America was identified with capitalism, and capitalism with evil. What was less rational was their wholesale swallowing of the most flagrant and stupid lies about American society and foreign policy, and their careful spurning of accurate knowledge of the Communist systems. An irrational anti-Americanism, with a blind rejection of factual and verifiable information about America and its antidemocratic enemies, was even more paradoxical among those sectors of Western opinion—the majority, in fact—who feared and rejected Communism. (At the beginning of the twenty-first century, they are rising above the former prejudice.) On the other hand, the ant-Americanism of the Right and even the extreme Right, as blindly passionate as the Left's though with a different rationale, is characteristically a French phenomenon.

3

The European Right's anti-Americanism stems fundamentally from our continent's loss during the twentieth century of its six-hundred-year leadership role. Europe had been the powerhouse of enterprise and industry, innovator in arts and sciences, maker of empires—in practical terms, master of the planet. It was sometimes one European country, sometimes another, that took the lead in this process of globalization *avant la lettre,* but all more or less participated, either in concert or by turns. Today, by contrast, not only has Europe lost the ability to act alone on a global scale, but it is compelled in some degree to follow in the footsteps of the United States and lend support. It is in France that this loss—real or imaginary—of great-power status engenders the most bitterness. As for the anti-Americanism of the extreme Right, it is fueled by the same hatred for democracy and the liberal economy that goads the extreme Left.*

As the sixties unfolded, I had begun to be invaded by doubts as to the validity of this reflexive anti-Americanism, which indiscriminately condemned America's "imperialistic" foreign policy—Soviet imperialism, in contrast, was but philanthropy—and American society. When I traveled to America in the early winter of 1969 to research *Without Marx or Jesus,* I was astonished by evidence that everything Europeans were saying about the U.S. was false. Over the course of a few weeks I went from the East Coast to the West Coast, with a stay in Chicago along the way. Rather than a conformist society, what I found was one in the throes of political, social and cultural upheaval.

The French like to imagine themselves the inventors, in May 1968, of the kind of political protest that had been inflaming American universities and minorities for several years already. Not only had their antiestablishment movement gathered momentum well before ours, but the authorities whose legitimacy was challenged had responded in a far more democratic way than ours. Moreover, their dissidents, while guilty of follies of their own, continued to try out fresh ideas; ours, on the other

---

*A typical example, from among other publications of the same sort, is the autumn 1996 issue of *Identité*—the "Revue of National Studies." The cover shouts: "AMERICA: ENEMY OF THE PEOPLE." An article informs us that America is bent upon "enslaving the world" by means, particularly, of NATO and the WTO. Note the striking similarity between this paranoid propaganda and left-wing themes pumped out by antiglobalists in Seattle and Genoa. And for Le Pen's National Front, the American constitutional republic is really a totalitarian state. It's clear that LePenism, leftism and warmed-over Maoism share a common enthusiasm: hatred for the U.S.A.

hand, rapidly lost whatever originality they had, regressing into tired ideological molds of the past—notably Maoism—then sinking to the depths
of fanatical and murderous terrorism, above all in Germany and Italy.

I was struck by the vast gulf that separated our state-controlled television news services—stilted, long-winded and monotonous, dedicated
to presenting the official version of events—from the lively, aggressive
evening news shows on NBC or CBS, crammed with eye-opening images
and reportage that offered unflinching views of social and political realities at home and American involvement abroad. Vietnam was their principal target, of course, and public opinion was turning increasingly against
the war, a turnaround the media were largely responsible for. And this
was the society that Europeans, looking down from the heights of their
uninformed prejudices, described as a society of censorship.

I was also pleasantly surprised by the conversations I had with a wide
range of Americans—politicians, journalists, businessmen, students and
university professors, Democrats and Republicans, conservatives, liber-
als and radicals, and people I met in passing from every walk of life.
Whereas in France people's opinions were fairly predictable and tended
to follow along lines laid down by their social role, what I heard in America was much more varied—and frequently unexpected. I realized that
many more Americans than Europeans had formed their own opinions
about matters—whether intelligent or idiotic is another question—rather
than just parroting the received wisdom of their social milieu.

In short, the United States I had discovered was in complete contrast to the conventional portrayal then generally accepted in Europe. It
was the clash between the mental image of the United States I had taken
as baggage from France and the reality I encountered that led to *Without Marx or Jesus.*

Even without leaving France, I realized, it required little investigative labor to demonstrate the falsity of the crudest arguments in the anti-
American repertory. Wasn't it obvious, for example, that it was Americans
themselves, led by Republicans, who in less than four years discredited
the bothersome Senator McCarthy? And didn't Soviet espionage in fact
allow Moscow to gain several years in the development of atomic weapons?
It has been more than amply confirmed—it was already proved in 1970—
that Julius and Ethel Rosenberg were indeed agents for the Comintern,
with the most harmful consequences; and that Alger Hiss, a close advisor to Franklin D. Roosevelt, notably at the Yalta Conference, also worked

for the East Bloc and passed information on to Stalin. For a long time whitewashed as martyrs of anticommunist hysteria, these traitors and many others have found the place in history that they justly deserve, at least in the eyes of those who respect historical truth.

Or again, however astonishing it may seem half a century later, Soviet propaganda, thanks to its echo chamber in the free but credulous world, succeeded for years in persuading millions of people that it was South Korea that had attacked North Korea in 1950 and not the reverse. Picasso himself signed on to the swindle when he painted *Massacre in Korea,* which depicts a squad of American soldiers opening fire on a group of women and naked children—thereby demonstrating that artistic genius need not be incompatible with moral ignominy. (The massacres could only have been perpetrated by Americans, of course, since it was well known that any acts that might jeopardize human life were deeply distasteful to Joe Stalin and Kim Il Sung.) Let me mention also for the record the farcical allegation of bacteriological warfare waged by Americans in Korea, a lie made up on the spot by a Soviet agent, the Australian journalist Wilfred Burchett. The astonishing thing is not that it was cooked up, but that even outside Communist circles it could gain a certain credibility—and this in countries where the press is free and it is easy to crosscheck data. The mystery of anti-Americanism is not the disinformation—reliable information on the United States has always been easy to obtain—but people's willingness to be disinformed.

Anti-Americanism increased tenfold by 1969 as a result of the war in Vietnam. But Europeans, and above all the French, with remarkable unfairness forgot or pretended to forget that the war was a direct offshoot of European colonial expansion in general, and of the French Indochina War in particular. Because France in her blindness had refused to decolonize after 1945; because she had rashly become involved in a distant and protracted war in the course of which she had, moreover, frequently pleaded for and sometimes obtained American help; because France, humiliatingly routed at the battle of Dien Bien Phu, was forced in 1954 to sign the disastrous Geneva Accords, handing over the northern half of Vietnam to a Communist regime that promptly violated the agreements: it was thus unquestionably only after a long series of political blunders and military setbacks on the part of France and the French that the United States was induced to intervene.

So unfolded a scenario that repeatedly is to be found underlying geostrategic and psychological relations between Europe and America. To begin with, Europeans entreat a reticent United States to rush to their aid and become actively involved in, even sponsor and coordinate, an effort to save them from a desperate situation that they, the Europeans, have created. Subsequently, America is transmuted into the sole instigator of the conflict. Needless to say, should America prove successful, as she did in the all-embracing challenge of the Cold War, she receives but scant acknowledgment. But should the affair turn bad, as it did in Vietnam, America bears all the blame.

In *Without Marx or Jesus* I spelled out numerous examples of the intrinsically contradictory character of passionate anti-Americanism. In this book I'd like to extend that list, so little has the syndrome changed over thirty years.

The illogicality at base consists in reproaching the United States for some shortcoming, and then for its opposite. Here is a convincing sign that we are in the presence, not of rational analysis, but of obsession. The examples I mentioned were from the sixties, but others can easily be adduced from much earlier and much later, revealing a deeply rooted habit of mind that hasn't altered in the slightest over the years. The lessons that can be drawn from the last three decades of the century, which hardly reflect badly on the United States, have apparently made no impression.

As an hors d'oeuvre, let me offer a particularly flagrant manifestation of this mentality, on display as I write these lines in September 2001. Until May of 2001, and for some years now, the main grievance against the United States was formulated in terms of the hyperpower's "unilateralism," its arrogant assumption that it could meddle everywhere and be the "policeman of the world." Then, over the summer of 2001, it became apparent that the administration of George W. Bush was less inclined than its predecessors to impose itself as universal lifesaver in one crisis after another—especially in the Middle East, where the conflict between the Israelis and the Palestinians was heating up alarmingly. From then on the reproof mutated into that of "isolationism": a powerful country failing in its duties and, with monstrous egocentricity, looking only to its own national interests. With wonderful illogicality, the same spiteful bad temper inspired both indictments, though of course they were diametrically opposed.

This contradiction reminded me of an argument made by General de Gaulle, who, in order to justify France's 1966 withdrawal from military participation in NATO, adduced the United States' tardiness in coming to France's aid in both World Wars. And yet that was precisely the purpose, in the light of past experiences, of the North Atlantic Treaty Organization: to guarantee the automatic and immediate military intervention on the part of the United States (and the other signatories) in case of aggression against one or another member state. Emotional prejudice can blind even a great man to the inherent absurdity of some of his positions. Alain Peyrefitte, in his *C'était de Gaulle,* quotes the general as saying: "In 1944, the Americans cared no more about liberating France than did the Russians about liberating Poland." When one knows how the Russians treated Poland, both during the last phase of World War II (holding back the Red Army's advance so as to give the Germans enough time to massacre the inhabitants of Varsovic), and then after they had made a satellite of the country, one cannot but be dumbfounded by the effrontery of such a comparison, coming from such a source.

But a third of a century later, we witnessed far worse. After the terrorist attacks of September 11, 2001, the vast majority of French people willingly joined in the three minutes of silence observed throughout the country to honor the memory of the thousands killed. Among those who didn't were the delegates and militants of the CGT (Confédération Générale du Travail) trade union during the weekend *L'Humanité* celebrations of September 15 and 16. Then, during the following weekend, it was the turn of the followers of Jean-Marie Le Pen's National Front, assembled for their traditional Bleu-Blanc-Rouge festival. So, gathered together under the banner of anti-Americanism, whatever their particular ideological mantras—and even, apparently, when antagonists—were all the xenophobes, all the partisans of backward and repressive regimes, not excluding the antiglobalists and pseudo-Greens.

In September 2001, the nadir of intellectual incoherence was achieved. (Let's not bother with the moral dimensions; we're too blasé for that.) After the first gushings of emotion and crocodile condolences, the murderous assaults were depicted as a justified retaliation for the evil done by the United States throughout the world. This was the reaction of most Muslim countries, but also of rulers and journalists in some sub-Saharan African countries, not all of which have Muslim majorities. Here we see the habitual escape hatch of societies suffering from chronic failure,

8

societies that have completely messed up their evolution toward democracy and economic growth; instead of looking to their own incompetence and corruption as the cause, they finger the West in general and the United States in particular. Classic displays of voluntary blindness to one's own shortcomings though these were, they were but overtures; even more remarkable performances were to come. After a discreet pause of a few days, the theory of American culpability surfaced in the European press—in France above all, it goes without saying—among intellectuals and politicians, of the Left and the Right.

Shouldn't we interrogate ourselves about the underlying reasons, the "root causes" that had pushed the terrorists to their destructive acts? Wasn't the United States in part responsible for what had happened? Shouldn't we take into account the sufferings of the poor countries and the contrast between their impoverishment and America's opulence?

This line of argument was not only made in countries whose populations, keyed up to fever pitch by jihad, instantly acclaimed the New York catastrophe as well-deserved punishment. It was also heard in the European democracies, where soon enough, insinuations were made that—with all due respect for the dead, of course—a careful look at the terrorists' motives was called for.

Here are shades of elementary Marxist cant, parroted by the enemies of globalization, according to which the wealthy are eternally accruing more riches at the expense of the poor, who are mired ever more deeply in poverty. Thus Marx believed he could predict that, in the industrialized countries he studied, capital was destined to become increasingly concentrated in the hands of an ever-smaller class of super-rich proprietors, who would be confronted by ever-increasing hordes of impoverished proletarians.

Put to the test, the theory was revealed as incorrect, for class relations within the developed societies simply did not go that way; likewise for the relations between the developed and the so-called developing nations. But inability to explain the facts has never prevented a theory from prospering, provided it is sustained by ideology and shielded by ignorance. As usual, facts are trumped by psychological imperatives.

A further step was quickly taken in the direction of intellectual decline when declarations multiplied demanding that the United States not launch a war against terrorism that could cause the entire planet to suffer. A gang of suicidal fanatics, indoctrinated, trained and financed by a powerful and rich multinational terrorist organization—or organizations—had murdered three thousand people in the heart of Manhattan, yet it was the victim who had mysteriously become the aggressor.

America's mistake was to try to defend herself and eradicate terrorism, according to the America-haters. Obsessed by their hatred and floundering in illogicality, these dupes forget that the United States, acting in her own self-interest, is also acting in the interest of us Europeans and in the interest of many other countries threatened, or already subverted and ruined, by terrorism.

Inevitably then, today as yesterday and yesterday as the day before, a book about the United States must be a book dealing with disinformation about the United States—a formidable and perhaps Sisyphean task of persuasion, doomed to failure, since the disinformation in question is not the result of pardonable, correctable mistakes, but rather of a profound psychological need. The mechanism of the Great Lie* that fences in America on every front, and the rejection of everything that might refute it, evokes the equivalent lie that surrounded the Soviet Union ever since 1917—not to the detriment, but to the advantage of the Communist empire. Here again, among those who fed from the idealized and falsified images of "existing socialism," a sort of mental flyswatter swiped away at facts that were too threateningly real.

During my time in the United States in 1969, I identified what I believed could fairly be called a revolution. In its narrow sense, "revolution" usually means the replacing of one political regime by another, usually by means of a violent coup d'état accompanied by insurrection—followed by purges, arrests and executions. Indeed, many a revolution conforming to this pattern has led to dictatorship and repression. As I stressed in *Without Marx or Jesus,* what I meant by "revolution" in the context of America was less a political phenomenon at the highest levels of power than a series of transformations spontaneously occurring within society at a deep level. These radical changes had been born, were evolving and would continue to evolve independently of political transitions at the national level. You can change the government without changing society; conversely, you can change society without

---

*The phrase comes from Ante Ciliga's title for his well-known book about the Soviet Union, *Au pays du grand mensonge,* originally published in 1940. An English translation is *The Russian Enigma* (Routledge, 1989).

changing the government. The American Free Speech Movement sprang forth and continued to grow as vigorously under Republican presidents as under Democrats; it was able to do so largely because it never—or very rarely—regressed into the backward ideologies of the nineteenth century or the Marxist pseudo-revolutionary theoretical straitjackets of the twentieth. In my book, I argued that a revolution in this sense is a phenomenon that had hitherto never taken place, an event that would develop along lines other than the known historical ones and that could not be thought about—or even perceived—in terms of the old categories. It was obvious to me that the real revolution was taking place not in Cuba, but in California.

The side-by-side comparison I had carried out, a stark confrontation between what was everywhere said about the United States and what one actually encountered upon going there, inspired my frontline report, which apparently resonated with many people throughout the world. *Without Marx or Jesus* was a bestseller in France and in the United States, taking off spectacularly before it came to the notice of the critics and continuing to stay aloft even after lukewarm, even hostile reviews; it was translated into at least twenty languages. This landslide revealed the gulf between the desire to know on the part of the "silent majorities" and the desire not to know on the part of the intellectual and media elites, not only in countries like France, Italy and Greece that were under overt Communist influence, but in social democracies like Sweden that were theoretically opposed to totalitarianism.

My Swedish publisher, a bon vivant and crawfish connoisseur, invited me to help with the book's launching in Stockholm. He wasn't able to get a single television appearance for me, which evidently didn't hurt sales in the slightest. In Finland, I was confronted by two delegations of apparatchiks—psychologically rigid Communist "intellectuals"—one from Romania, the other from Poland. The German author Hans-Magnus Enzenberger, trying to maintain the debate at a civilized level, spoke supportively on my behalf, even though his own contributions were violent critiques of American "imperialism." My Greek publisher was masochistic enough to compose (without, by the way, consulting or notifying me) a preface in which he begged pardon from his compatriots for having published in their language such a farrago of errors and imbecilities. When I ventured a timid protest, he called me a bigot. The *Corriere della sera,* while bestowing qualified approval on me, reported on the indignant brouhaha in France and Italy that my thesis, so outrageously unfashionable as it was, had caused. And my Italian translator sprinkled his version with footnotes reproving my ideas. I had fun congratulating him in an article I titled *Il traduttore bollente* ("The Enraged Translator"). To judge from the international success of my book, one must conclude that some attacks seem calculated to win readers rather than frighten them off. Their curiosity aroused, readers say to themselves that the author must be getting something right or he could never have provoked such a panicked, over-the-top response.

The Left saw clearly what was at issue: my book was less about America and anti-Americanism than about the epic twentieth-century struggle between socialism and liberal democracy, and they feared that chances for victory might be starting to lean in liberalism's favor. The principal function of anti-Americanism has always been, and still is, to discredit liberalism by discrediting its supreme incarnation. To travesty the United States as a repressive, unjust, racist—even fascist—society was a way of proclaiming: Look what happens when liberalism is implemented! And when I described the United States as not only a classical democratic system that worked rather better than any other, but as a society undergoing a revolutionary mutation upsetting its traditional values, the message was interpreted as an annoying wake-up call for the elites as they slumbered in their ideological easy chair—including those in the United States, where anti-Americanism continues to flourish in university, journalistic and literary circles. The Blame America First reflex to each and every problem has for long been instinctive among the cultural upper echelons.

When, on November 7, 1972, Richard Nixon was reelected president, crushing George McGovern, his left-of-center, "liberal" Democrat opponent, I became the target for various sneers: This triumph of a Republican—reputed to be of the Right—didn't it make my entire thesis utterly ridiculous? So much for my American revolution. Yet the central thesis of *Without Marx or Jesus* is this: The great revolution of the twentieth century will turn out to be the liberal revolution—by 1970 it was already patently obvious that the socialist revolution had failed everywhere. A series of chapters in the book establishes this failure in the countries of "actually existing" socialism (only too actual, alas); in Third World countries, which had believed that the key to development lay in socialist/interventionist recipes; and in the industrial democracies, where state control over the economy, under the pressure of reality, was being rolled back as the century closed and beyond.

The American liberal revolution was becoming the driving force behind what was to become known as "globalization" (or in French, *mondialisation,* which in my opinion is the more accurate term). Indeed, the subtitle of the French edition of *Without Marx or Jesus* is *From the Second American Revolution to the Second Global Revolution.* This liberal invasion of the world, which would triumph resoundingly above all after 1990 and the disintegration of Communism, is what Francis Fukuyama would call the End of History, an expression that has come in for some criticism because it has been poorly understood, especially by people who think they have read a book when they have only read its title.

So *Without Marx or Jesus* focused chiefly on the United States as a laboratory for the liberal-democratic solution. In each period, or at least in each period that is marked by progress, there exists what one might call a "laboratory society" where civilization's great inventions are tested. Not all are necessarily blessings, but they irresistibly prevail. Other nations have to adapt to these innovations, whether they like it or not. Athens, Rome, Renaissance Italy, eighteenth-century England and France—all were societies of this type, not as a result of some abstract "process," but because of human deeds. In the twentieth century, it was the turn of the United States. Hence it is not without reason, even if obviously overblown, that for billions of people the spread of the liberal economy is synonymous with Americanization.

It is the advent of this historical development that I attempted to describe in *Without Marx or Jesus.* To what extent is its flowering attributable only to America and her "hyperpower"? Was her role as "laboratory society" voluntarily or involuntarily assumed? Does she owe it to her "imperialism," her "unilateralism," or her vigorous capacity for innovation? Has the American solution created—or at least to an equal extent been created by—a universal need? These are the questions I shall try to answer.

1. Contradictions

THERE HAVE BEEN POWERS and empires on an international scale in the past, long before the United States at the beginning of the twenty-first century. But never before has a power attained global supremacy, a state of affairs examined by Zbigniew Brzezinski, Jimmy Carter's national security advisor, in his book *The Grand Chessboard.** To merit the title of "global superpower," a country must rank first in four domains: economic, technological, military and cultural. America is the first nation in history to do so. Economically, from the recovery of 1983 to the beginning of recession in 2000, she leapt ahead, combining steady growth with virtually full employment, a balanced budget (for the first time in thirty years) and very low inflation. In technology, especially since the lightning progress made in the field of communications technologies, she enjoyed a quasi monopoly. And militarily, she alone can project overwhelming power anywhere in the world, at any time.

The question of cultural superiority is more debatable, depending on whether "culture" is narrowly or broadly defined. In the more limited sense, with reference to high culture in the realms of literature, painting, music and architecture, American civilization is certainly outstanding, but it does not stand alone and its influence cannot be compared to that of ancient Greece, of Rome, of China. One of the reasons is that American artistic and literary culture has a tendency towards provincialism: English is dominant globally, and fewer and fewer Americans feel any

---

* *The Grand Chessboard: American Primacy and Its Geostrategic Imperatives* (Basic Books, 1997).

need to read in other languages. And when American universities and critics take up foreign schools of thought, they too often obey the dictates of faddish conformism rather than exercise independent judgment.

On the other hand, Brzezinski is incontestably right when it comes to the broader connotation. America's popular culture, skillfully advertised, reaches the entire world via the new high-tech media, and American tastes—in dress, music, recreation and fast food—attract young people everywhere. American movies and television shows draw audiences of millions, so much so that some countries (including France, naturally) seek to establish protectionist barriers in the name of "cultural exceptionalism." English has become the de facto language of the Internet and has for a long time been the international language of science. A sizeable proportion of the political, technological and scientific elites throughout the world have graduated from American universities.

Even more decisive (with all due deference to socialists past and present) has been the victory of the liberal-democratic model as a result of the demise of Communism. Likewise, American-style federalist democracy is increasingly being imitated, starting with the European Union; it serves as the organizing principle of international alliances such as NATO and the United Nations. This is not to deny the flaws of the American system, its lapses and hypocrisies. But the fact remains that Asia, Africa and Latin America have little to teach the United States about democracy. And as for Europe, let's not forget that we invented the great criminal ideologies of the twentieth century, forcing the United States to intervene on our continent twice with her armies. America largely owes her unique superpower status today to Europe's mistakes.

Not so long ago, for example, France was reproaching the United States for wanting to displace her influence in Africa. But France bears a heavy responsibility for the genesis of the 1994 massacres in Rwanda and the subsequent disintegration of Zaire. France discredited herself without any help from anyone else, creating a vacuum that was to be filled by a growing United States presence.

The European Union is making scant progress towards the realization of a single decision-making center; it can be likened to a choir whose every member takes herself to be a soloist. Lacking unity, how can Europe counterbalance the effectiveness of America's foreign policy when planning the slightest undertaking requires first securing unanimity among fifteen nations? Or what about twenty-seven, and these even more disparate than today's membership?

Evidently, American ascendancy is indebted only in part to the creativity and determination of the American people; it also sprang by default from the cumulative failures of the rest of the world: the fall of Communism, the ruin of Africa, the divisions within Europe, the Asian and Latin American slowness to evolve towards democracy.

The word "superpower" seeming too weak and banal to him, in 1998 Hubert Védrine, the French minister of foreign affairs in the "plural Left" government, substituted the neologism "hyperpower." According to him, this word is stronger and more descriptive of the United States' present hegemony. One doesn't see quite why, since the Greek prefix "hyper" has exactly the same meaning as the Latin "super." But Mr. Védrine believes it better describes a country that is predominant in every category, including "attitudes, concepts, language, lifestyles." The prefix "hyper," he adds, is considered aggressive by the American media, but he insists there is nothing pejorative about it. Simply put, "We cannot accept a politically unipolar and culturally homogenized world, any more than the unilateralism of a single hyperpower." Which is a self-contradictory line of argument, since if "hyperpower" is not a pejorative term, why is the reality it points to unacceptable?

Acceptable or not, the fact is that it exists. And what is lacking in European thinking about the current state of affairs (and Europeans are far from being alone in this instance) is an enquiry into its primary causes. It is only by identifying and correctly interpreting these causes that we'll have a chance of finding ways to counterbalance the Americans' dominance.

Europeans in particular should force themselves to examine how they have contributed to that preponderance. It was they, after all, who made the twentieth century the darkest in history; it was they who brought about the two unprecedented cataclysms of the World Wars; and it was they who invented and put into place the two most criminal regimes ever inflicted on the human race—pinnacles of evil and imbecility achieved in a space of less than thirty years.

It is, again, Europe we must blame, at least partly, for the problematic legacy of colonialism in the Third World, for the impasses and convulsions of underdevelopment. It was the European nations—England, Belgium, Spain, France and Holland, and belatedly and to a lesser degree

Germany and Italy—who were bent on conquering and appropriating other continents. It won't do to bring up the extermination of the Native Americans or black slavery against the United States, for after all, who were the occupants of the future United States if not white colonizers from Europe? And from whom did these European colonists buy their slaves if not from European slave traders?

To the situation created by the suicidal World Wars and the European propensity to engender totalitarian regimes was added the obligation to develop the economic wasteland left by Communism after its collapse. Here again, Europe had little to propose by way of solutions. The political, cultural and media elites, for the most part, never really understood Communism (consider for a moment the praise heaped, even by the Right, on Mao Tse-tung during the worst moments of his destructive fanaticism), and they were intellectually ill-prepared to understand the process of its demise or to render assistance.* With regard to this additional and unprecedented problem, the current American "hyperpower" is the direct consequence of European powerlessness, both past and present. The United States fills a void caused by our inadequacy—not in our capabilities, but in our thinking and our will to act.

Consider, for example, the perplexity of a citizen of Montana or Tennessee upon learning of his nation's intervention in the former Yugoslavia. He might with good reason have asked himself what interest the United States could have in plunging into the bloody quagmire of the Balkans, that centuries-old masterpiece of Europe's matchless ingenuity. But Europe found herself incapable of bringing order to this murderous chaos of her own making. So, in order to stop or at least diminish the massacres, it devolved upon the United States to take charge of the operations in Bosnia, Kosovo and Macedonia. The Europeans afterwards offered thanks by calling them imperialists—although they quake with fright and accuse the Americans of being cowardly isolationists the moment they make the slightest mention of bringing their soldiers home.

■ ■ ■

SOME CRITICISMS REVEAL the weaknesses and fantasies of the critics rather than the errors of those they criticize. Certainly America, like all societies, has many defects and deserves any number of criticisms; but to

---

*I refer the reader to a previous book of mine, *Le Regain démocratique* (Fayard, 1992).

express something other than her detractors' phobias, these reproaches should target real defects. The pitying sniggers ritually directed against the American whipping boy by the European media, however, come for the most part from an ignorance so profound that it seems deliberate. On the other hand, confining ourselves to the period of the United States' emergence as sole superpower, dozens of serious books and hundreds of serious articles have been published, by American and European authors alike, dealing with America. In contrast to the run-of-the-mill obsessive complaints, this material makes available—for those who are willing to be informed—balanced and factual information about American civilization, its successes and failures, its good deeds and bad, its moments of clear vision and of blindness. And if harsh judgments can be found in this unbiased literature, we may at least feel confident that they are not dictated by incompetence. Laziness is not an adequate explanation for the ignorance of European opinion-makers; it must, more often than not, be voluntary and imputable to ruling *idées fixes*.

This intentional turning away from facts begins with sociological questions concerning the United States—the alleged absence of social protection and solidarity, the notorious "poverty line" (a phrase that's used haphazardly by people who obviously haven't the slightest idea about its technical meaning, as if this economic indicator had the same real value in Canada as in Zimbabwe), or even the unemployment level. Concerning this last, the fact that after 1984, unemployment in the United States fell to below 5 percent, whereas in France it shot up to 12 percent, implied nothing good about America, according to our commentators, because so many casual and entry-level jobs were included in the statistics. How well we have been reassured by the myth of the minimum-wage job!

At the time of the economic slowdown during the first half of 2001, unemployment in America climbed back from 4.4 percent to 5.5 percent. A typical response to this alarming state of affairs: "The End of Full Employment in the U.S.A." gleefully announced the front-page headline of the economics journal *La Tribune* of May 7, 2001. Yet this was at a time when the French government was frenetically heaping praises on itself for *reducing* unemployment levels to 8.7 percent—almost twice the American level (not counting the tens of thousands of the effectively unemployed who in France are artificially excluded from the statistics). By September 2001, unemployment in France had already climbed back to over 9 percent. But *Le Monde* (February 15, 2001) had published an article entitled "The End of the American Economic Dream." Thus, a practically uninterrupted economic growth over seventeen years (1983–2000), a technological revolution without precedent since the nineteenth century, the creation of tens of millions of new jobs, an unemployment level fallen to a little over 4 percent, a tremendous population increase (going from 248 to 281 million between 1990 and 2000), all this was but a "dream." If only France had dreamt that way! And then the article's author, getting on the "casual jobs" hobbyhorse, deplores how France has become Americanized to the point of "copying the sad example of the working poor," evidently the sole lesson to be learned from the American economy. France would doubtless have been better off remaining faithful to its model of "not-working poor."

We will come back to the disheartening catalogue drawn up by America's accusers; my aim here is simply to point out the intrinsically contradictory character of their diatribes. For if—according to their account—American civilization is nothing but an accumulation of economic, political, social and cultural calamities, how is it that the rest of the world is so worried about America's wealth, scientific and technological preeminence, and cultural ubiquity? The unfortunate nation of their imagination ought to evoke pity rather than envy, commiseration rather than dislike. Here is an enigma for us to contemplate: how America's success derives entirely from her abysmal inferiority and never, according to us, from her intrinsic merits.

After the social issues, it is the way American institutions work that we understand badly or don't want to understand. I'll mention only one example of this for the moment: the worldwide reaction, especially in Europe, of blended joy and scorn that greeted the long uncertainty about the result of the American presidential election of November 2000.

Many years ago, at the variety theater El Salón México (immortalized in Aaron Copland's orchestral composition of that name), I was entertained by a satirical sketch in which a Mexican *peón* and an American tourist are having a discussion. The American boasts of his nation's prowess, offering as an example:

"In the United States, three minutes after the polls have closed we know who the next president is."

"That's nothing, my friend!" the *péon* retorts. "In Mexico, we know it six months ahead of time."

And it's true that at the time—and for long afterwards—the Institutional Revolutionary Party (PRI) was monopolizing every instrument of power and was fixing all the elections. Each president was in effect appointing his successor.

How times have changed. In 2000, for the first time, a Mexican opposition party's candidate was able to win the presidency through honest electoral process. The result was not known in advance. So in Mexico, democracy has made incontestable progress.

In the same year, however, weeks passed before Americans knew who would next occupy the White House. Many foreign commentators thought the protracted cliffhanger after the election on November 7, 2000, showed that American democracy was in bad shape.

This crude misrepresentation misses the point: a tight election involving ballot recounts indicates the health of a democracy, not the reverse. It is in dictatorships, however disguised as legitimate electoral presidencies, that the victor carries the day with a colossal margin.

There are many ways to ensure efficient elections. France has a two-step method: only the two candidates who come out on top in the first round may participate in the second presidential vote. The English method of majority voting in a single round of elections for the House of Commons is especially brutal when there are numerous candidates for the same seat. A candidate could win the seat with one-quarter or one-third of the votes if that puts him at the top.

In comparison, the American system of the Electoral College seems much fairer. The number of electors is proportional to the population of each state. The candidate who surpasses 50 percent of the popular vote in a state gains all the electoral votes—just as in France a candidate gains all the presidential power in the second round even if 49.9 percent of the electorate voted against him, and no one contests his legitimacy. So why talk of elitism with regard to the American Electoral College system? By state law, though not by the Constitution, the electors are obliged to ratify the popular vote in 26 of the 50 states, as well as the District of Columbia. In 24 states the electors are legally free to select the minority candidate instead, but this has never happened since the beginning of the nineteenth century.

So when the rulers and intelligentsia of manifestly undemocratic countries see fit to call the United States a "banana republic," they are exhibiting their own bad faith; coming from a Muammar al-Qaddafi or a Robert Mugabe, card-carrying grave-diggers of democracy, such comments are amusing; while from the Russians, whose restoration of universal suffrage was indeed encouraging though fraught with problems, they are merely hypocritical. But it's hard not to laugh when one reads a remark like the following, from the pen of novelist Salman Rushdie: "India is doing better than the United States thanks to its electoral system of direct universal suffrage." Only Rushdie seems to be unaware that India beats all records when it comes to electoral fraud; we make a show of not noticing it, happy that India remains more or less a democracy.

What our European press has all along condescendingly called the American "soap opera" was essentially a constitutional process; and in the event of a tied election, the future president would be elected in the House of Representatives.

Disdainful comments were also heard, in Europe and elsewhere, about the Americans' recourse to the courts, which were required to decide about candidates' rights with regard to ballot recounts in the state of Florida. This legal wrangling over the issue of who would occupy the world's most visible post, they charged, was deplorable.

In reply, it could be argued that court rulings are altogether preferable to the rule of the streets. And throughout this critical period in the United States, despite the intensity of the polemics, there was no hint of violence in a confused state of affairs that would have provoked a coup d'état or a civil war in many another country.

Indeed, the ironical remarks made about American judges reveal a complete failure to comprehend the place of judicial power in the United States and its relation to political power. As long ago as 1835, Tocqueville wrote: "What a foreigner has the greatest difficulty in understanding about the United States is the judicial system. There is, so to speak, scarcely a political event where a judge's authority isn't invoked." Since political issues may be transformed in this way into judicial ones, foreigners often infer, even today, that in America judges are usurping political power. Tocqueville clearly shows why this is false. Indeed, the judiciary remains within the classical limits of its proper domain. There are three reasons for this: first, it functions always and solely as an arbitrator; second, it gives verdicts only in particular cases and not on questions about general principles; third, it can act only when appealed to.

It is therefore erroneous to prattle about a "government by judges." Judges may not act as substitutes for the executive or legislative branches.

What is true is that, institutionally as well as attitudinally, the law takes precedence over the state. Yet it is only through interpreting the law that the judiciary can act politically, and only if someone asks it to.

Democracy in the European Union works far less well than in the United States. The voting weight of each European country in the European Parliament and the Commission bears only a remote connection to its relative demographic weight. Out of the fifteen member countries, the ten least populated have together a population equivalent to Germany's, but in the Council of Ministers they have thirty-nine votes while Germany has only ten. In the Parliament, Germany has one Euro-MP per 1,200,000 or so inhabitants, whereas Luxembourg has one per 67,000 inhabitants. The Nice summit of December 2000 merely skimmed over the problem of correcting these imbalances. Clearly the Europeans have been less successful than the Americans in finding an equitable compromise between the political claims of the smallest and the largest states.

■ ■ ■

THE MISREPRESENTATIONS OF social relations and living standards in the United States, while gratifying anti-American passions, serve finally to denigrate free market economies. Likewise, the incomprehension or caricaturing of American institutions helps to spread the idea that the United States is not truly a democracy, and, by extrapolation, that liberal democracies are democratic in appearance only. But it's in the area of international relations that the "hyperpower" finds itself held in particular abhorrence.

Let me be clear about this: American foreign policy certainly and in many respects deserves criticism; and here American journalists are eager to show themselves in the forefront. Such critiques, even when they are not entirely convincing, are legitimate and useful, provided they rest on a degree of rational analysis. But when Vladimir Putin asserts with impressive assurance that it was NATO's (read: America's) "crimes" in Kosovo, and Slobodan Milosevic's appearance before the International Court of Justice in 2001, that "destabilized" Yugoslavia (which country has needed no help in the business of destabilization), we are hearing not a rational critique, but a deliberate lie or a self-contradictory hallucination—clearly the old mistake of confusing cause and effect. The purpose of this exercise is perhaps psychological: to flatter Slavic self-esteem. Yet its political utility, for all parties concerned, is negligible. If by resorting to fables of this sort, Putin hopes to restore "great power" status to Russia, then he will quickly be brought back to earth; effective action cannot proceed from faulty analysis. If Russia is not a superpower at the beginning of the twenty-first century, that's because she embarked on the absurd experiment of Communism, which left her much more backward than before 1917. It is by facing up to this reality that Russia will be able to surmount her backwardness, not by putting the United States on trial at every turn.

The European Union, and by extension the whole "international community" (as it is ironically called), also rushed headlong into a fog of consolatory, narcissistic futility as they addressed the first foreign policy initiatives of George W. Bush at the beginning of his presidency. For the time being I'll limit myself to one example of this: the international reactions to President Bush's refusal to confirm his predecessor's commitments—purely platonic, by the way—with regard to the environment.

In 1997, under the aegis of the United Nations, delegates from 168 countries gathered in Kyoto to sign a protocol designed to reduce emissions of greenhouse gases. But in January 2001, shortly after taking office, George W. Bush withdrew American adherence to the Kyoto Protocol. Forthwith there was an eruption of indignation, even insults, mainly from Europe. It was loudly proclaimed that Bush was cynically sacrificing the planet's future for capitalist profit, and especially for the profit of the petroleum industry, whose notorious lackey he was. Unfortunately, the authors of this shrewd analysis overlooked some easily ascertainable facts.

Already in 1997, with Bill Clinton occupying the White House, the U.S. Senate had rejected the Kyoto Protocol by a vote of 95 to 0—whether rightly or wrongly is another question. The fact remains that George W. Bush had nothing to do with it. Then Clinton, just before handing over power to his successor, had signed an executive order restoring United States support for the famous protocol. Customarily, such executive orders at the end of a president's term of office do not impinge on questions of high importance to national policy. Here, Clinton's evident intention was to hand Bush a political hot potato at the last minute. If he accepted it, the incoming president would be faced with the problem of reducing greenhouse gas emissions by 5.2 percent without cutting back industrial production and energy consumption too drastically: an impossible task. If he refused, noisy protests would surely be launched worldwide against him, protests all the more hypocritical in that those who cried the loudest, banishing the United States from the family of humanity in the name of environmental ethics, were careful not to apply this standard to themselves. By mid-2001, four years after the Kyoto conference, not one of the 167 other signatories—and not a single European nation—had ratified the protocol.

For the time being I'll lay aside the question of whether the Kyoto Protocol was a realistic program—and whether, in fact, global warming has been scientifically verified. I will simply point out the double standard when nations that are heavy polluters—such as Brazil, China and India—demand that the United States apply restrictions that they themselves don't feel required to observe. In a report published on May 29, 2001, the European Environment Agency noted a worsening of pollution in Europe, mainly because "transportation is constantly increasing, in particular those modes that are least sustainable (road and air)." The agency also noted air pollution increases from domestic heating and water pollution from nitrates. The sermonizers show little inclination to set a good example.

From there to the idea of an anti-American psychopathology, which routinely seeks to transform the United States into a scapegoat burdened with all the sins of the world, is a small and rather tempting step. Ecologists will reply that this is wrong, that America, with 5 percent of the world's population, is responsible for 25 percent of the world's industrial pollution. Perhaps the figures are accurate; but it should be pointed out that America also produces 25 percent of the planet's goods and services, and that the other 167 Kyoto signatories had done absolutely nothing by mid-2001 towards reducing, either collectively or individually, their 75 percent share of world pollution. Here is utter inconsistency, of course, but the agenda is less about ridding the world of pollution than about excommunicating the United States.

Whatever reproaches American environmental policy may (or may not) deserve, it's clear that the crux of the debate is situated elsewhere. The environmentalists' agenda is to set up the United States, which is to say capitalism, as the supreme culprit, indeed the sole culprit, behind worldwide pollution and the supposed warming of the atmosphere. For our Western environmentalists are hardly objective scientists: they are leftists. They are interested in the environment only insofar as they can exploit it as an issue to attack liberal societies.

During the seventies and eighties, they never denounced pollution in the Communist countries, a thousand times worse than in the West—

but after all, that wasn't capitalist pollution. They maintained a prudent silence at the time of the Chernobyl accident, as they do today with regard to the dilapidated nuclear power plants strewn over the erstwhile Communist territories. And they keep their mouths shut about the hundreds of Soviet-built submarines, stuffed with atomic warheads, that the Russians sank lock, stock and barrel in the Barents Sea.

To demand that steps be taken to rid humanity of this mortal peril that will hang over our heads for millennia would, from their socialist point of view, be inadvisable. After all, this tedious chore wouldn't be of the slightest help in their crusade against liberal globalization, in their eyes a far more dreadful curse. Once upon a time there was a genuine environmentalism, which flourished in the sixties, precisely in the United States. But it has long since been hijacked by a mendacious pseudo-environmentalism, a mask for stale Marxist cant colored in green. Note that ideological environmentalism sees nature menaced only in those nations where economic liberty reigns to a greater or lesser degree—and above all, of course, in the most prosperous of them all.

If the Green parties were honestly aiming at practical results, they would begin by endeavoring to make every country reduce its energy consumption by the draconian 5.2 percent that was agreed upon at Kyoto. It's up to them, and especially those with positions in government, to convince majorities to cut freeway speed limits in half and energy requirements for private dwellings by one-third, not to mention inevitable billing surcharges for energy consumption over established ceilings. But to recommend such a drastic program without reservation and to implement it rapidly would inevitably expose the Greens and their allies to sharp electoral setbacks. Reason enough, as a substitute for action, to castigate the United States.

Thus France, which had Green ministers for five long years under the Jospin government (1997–2002), adopted none of the measures to protect the environment that a courageous policy would have called for: among them the banning of nitrates, for example, which would have done much to prevent water pollution but would have provoked a revolt among small farmers; or the "ecotax," which would have put to flight the vote of many a weary taxpayer. The authorities do not even try to enforce the speed limits that are presently in place, liberal though they currently are; what likelihood, then, that they would legislate for sterner rules? Was it the United States that prevented the French government from beginning to implement the Kyoto process, which provided for a 5.2 percent drop in energy consumption (from the 1990 level) to be achieved by 2012?

On May 31, 2002, the fifteen member nations of the European Union finally, after a delay of five years, ratified the Kyoto Protocol; we'll see if there's any serious attempt to put it into effect within the allotted time.

Equivocal posturing of this sort is made much easier, as I have already pointed out, by a refusal to acknowledge facts—or by an unscrupulous willingness to fabricate spurious data. One example of this was the reception accorded the United States National Academy of Sciences' report of June 2001, the product of several years of measurements, on climate change. The results were immediately presented by the media as a shout of alarm confirming the eco-leftists' worst anxieties about global warming. First into the ring was CNN, which proclaimed that the report was a "unanimous decision that global warming is real, is getting worse, and is due to man. There is no wiggle room."*

This version of the scientists' conclusions was repeated by a large part of the press on both sides of the Atlantic. Such gross falsifications roused the Academy of Sciences to publish a clarification spelling out exactly what the report did and did not say.

What the report actually emphasized was that twenty years is too short a period to evaluate long-term trends with any certainty; what *can* be stated with certainty is the following:

1. The average rise in global temperature was one-half degree over the past century.
2. Carbon dioxide levels in the atmosphere have been rising over the past two centuries.
3. Carbon dioxide does generate a greenhouse effect, but a less significant one than that of water vapor and clouds.

Above all, the Academy concluded, nothing allows us to ascribe climatic change to carbon dioxide or to predict which way the climate will go in the future; and in fact, thirty years ago it was planetary *cooling* that was the main concern of climatologists.

This clarification by the American scientists was deliberately ignored. For example, *The Economist,* a weekly magazine internationally respected for its reliability, published in its June 16, 2001, issue an article entitled

---

* *Wall Street Journal,* 12 June 2001.

"Burning Bush." With superb indifference to the Academy's previously released denial, the article repeated the lie that a "recent report of the U.S. National Academy of Sciences confirms the reality of global warming."*

■ ■ ■

THUS THE UNITED STATES is always blamed, while its financial and military aid are universally desired. For example at the June 2001 meeting of the Organization of African Unity at Lusaka, Zambia, African leaders hoped and prayed for a "Marshall Plan for Africa." This reference to the Marshall Plan of course evokes the historic precedent, financed by the United States, that brought Europe back out of the ruins of the Second World War. And yet virtually all of the mendicant chiefs who "govern" Africa profess a virulent anti-Americanism; culpability for the continent's poverty, and even the African AIDS epidemic, is laid at America's door. Anti-Americanism thus functions as a blame-shifting tactic. In fact, the international aid received by Africa since decolonization is equivalent to four or five Marshall Plans, all of which was squandered, embezzled or outright stolen, when it wasn't swallowed up in incessant wars or wiped out in stupid "agrarian reforms" modeled on the suffocating collectivism of Russia and China. But it's convenient to throw back on America all responsibility for one's own mistakes or crimes—while still appealing to her for rescue.

Europe is not exempt from this doublethink: at the very time when Europeans were benefiting from the Marshall Plan, leftist parties were opposed to it, putting it down as an American plot to put Western Europe under her thumb—yet another neocolonialist and imperialist maneuver, as could easily be deduced from Marxist theory. Yet the socialist or Christian-Democratic parties of the center-right that were then in power in most European countries also eschewed any feelings of gratitude, reasoning that by acting generously, America was acting purely in her own interests—as if she really ought to have opposed them! For Americans to have understood that it was to their own advantage to aid Europe's economic

---

*For reconsiderations of the entire question of global warming, see Le Progrès et ses ennemis (Fayard, 2001); and Bjorn Lomborg, The Skeptical Environmentalist (Cambridge University Press, 2001). (It should be noted that The Economist subsequently published an editorial piece giving strong support to Lomborg.)

recovery was not credited to their political intelligence. In keeping with the habitually contradictory rules of anti-American reasoning, we accused and keep accusing Americans of being opposed to a strong Europe; hence, the United States strengthens Europe because she wants to weaken Europe. In this regard, European thinking is a model of coherence.

The world should take note that America, for the time being, is the sole power at once capable of saving Mexico from economic collapse (in 1995); dissuading Communist China from attacking Taiwan; mediating between India and Pakistan in the matter of Kashmir; pressuring the Serb government to compel Slobodan Milosevic to appear before the International Court of Justice at The Hague; and working with some chance of success towards the reunification of the two Koreas under a democratic regime. The European Union did try to become involved in this last problem by sending a delegation, headed by the Swedish prime minister, to Pyongyang in May 2001. They could find nothing better to do than grovel before Kim Jong Il, the criminal chief of one of the last totalitarian jails on the planet. The European "solution" is apparently for South Korea to fall into line with North Korea, and not vice versa. If the Europeans believe they can put an end to the United States' "unilateralism" with inspired thinking like this, American diplomatic primacy could well remain with us for a long time.

The unilateralism in question arises automatically from the weakness of the other powers, a weakness more often intellectual than material; that is, it stems from faulty analysis rather than inadequate economic, political and strategic resources. Nothing, for example, prevented the Europeans from joining forces with the Americans as the latter went to the aid of the Afghan resistance fighters in their struggle against the invading Soviets in the 1980s. It was not for want of means that they sat on the fence, but from obsequiousness towards the Soviet Union and obedience to a lamentable geopolitical analysis, whose chief priority was "safeguarding détente"—as if détente were not by then well and truly dead, and as if it had ever existed apart from naïvely optimistic Western fantasies.

A similar confusion pervades attitudes towards economic realities. On the one hand, Americans are reproached for wanting to "impose their economic and social model on others." On the other, when there is a slowdown of the American economy, the rest of the world sooner or later begins to suffer the consequences, and then everyone anxiously awaits an American "recovery," counting on their own economies to follow in tandem. Consequently one can't help being a little perplexed: how can such an undesirable economy, whose formula supposedly no one wants to copy, be capable of functioning as both the motor and the brake of the world economy?

It's understandable that the Americans, confronted by such a host of inconsistencies, are sometimes tempted to think of themselves as crusaders invested with a kind of universal mission; this is why their spokesmen are not unlikely to indulge in irritating, obnoxious or comical remarks, sometimes verging on megalomania. This unfortunate tendency calls for some comment.

First, such remarks—however over-the-top—have a basis in indisputable fact. Second, thousands of equally grotesque statements have issued from French mouths, celebrating, over the course of the centuries, the "universal radiance" of France, the "country of human rights," burdened with the responsibility of spreading liberty, equality and fraternity throughout the world. Likewise, the Soviet Union regarded itself as the bearer of universal revolution, while Muslims want to force even non-Muslim countries to obey the *sharia*.

Third, the concept of a state policy, or *realpolitik,* indifferent alike to morality and the interests of others was discredited as a principle of international politics after the First World War. It was replaced by the principle of collective security, brought to Europe from the United States by Woodrow Wilson in 1919 and strongly reaffirmed by Franklin Roosevelt and Harry Truman in 1945.

The style of international politics inspired by this principle is an American invention and has been played out since 1945 under American leadership; it's hard to see what other approach could take us towards a less flawed world. For the politics of collective security (which naturally includes the war on terrorism) not to give rise to American "hyperpower," many other countries must have the intelligence to work together towards its fulfillment, instead of slandering its foremost champion.

2. Antiglobalism and Anti-Americanism

HOW TO UNDERSTAND this war against globalization, which since 1999 has continued to grow in scope and virulence? It is a war in the real, not the figurative sense of the word; a physical, not a theoretical struggle, fought in the streets and not in the realm of ideas—for the demonstrators who are its shock troops, organized by nongovernmental organizations (themselves subsidized by governments), sack the cities and lay siege to the venues where international meetings are held.

It is hard to be hostile in principle to globalization, which means freedom of movement for goods and people. So behind the fight against it lies an older and more fundamental struggle against liberalism, whose chief representative and most powerful vehicle is the United States. In the antiglobalist carnival that took place in Montpellier on February 16, 2001, the parade's star attraction was an Uncle Sam in a Stars-and-Stripes costume with a tall hat and a goatee. It would be hard to point more clearly to the supreme scapegoat; for in the old socialist tradition, antiliberalism and anti-Americanism are impossible to separate. The protestors at Montpellier were surely card-carrying rank and file of the beaten Communist legions or their political heirs, who, when frontal combat in open country was no longer feasible, regrouped to wage a harassing guerrilla war—a war made possible worldwide by the very freedom of movement that accompanies globalization. A vague concept if ever there was one, globalism serves as their new target, but one through which they actually take aim at their eternal enemies.

Do I simplify or exaggerate? Not at all. At one London rally in support of the Seattle demonstrations against the World Trade Organization occurring at the same time, banners read: "PRIVATIZATION KILLS.

CAPITALISM KILLS." Would *Le Monde diplomatique* or Pierre Bour-
dieu contend otherwise? According to these people and their fellow believers, the global marketplace will breed ever-increasing poverty, for the profit
of an ever-richer minority. This is the outcome Karl Marx predicted in
the middle of the nineteenth century for the industrialized nations of
Western Europe and North America, and we all know how history has
confirmed that brilliant prophecy. By the late 1950s, the French Communist Party was still using the "complete pauperization" of the working class
as a propaganda line—even while the thirty-year boom following World
War II was in full swing. That's the genius of "scientific socialism."

Lionel Jospin greeted the antiglobalizers of Genoa, Göteborg, Nice
and Seattle as "the worldwide emergence of a socially aware movement."
But it is actually the resurgence of antidemocratic violence on the part
of a minority. Democracies allow everyone the right to demonstrate
peacefully, to march, to shout slogans and display opinions and demands
on placards. But since Seattle, the radicals have gone far beyond legitimate protest. Wherever they have been active, their goal from the beginning has been to *prevent* meetings of elected heads of state or appointed
officials of international organizations, or even, as at Davos, colloquies
for exchanging points of view but, as far as I know, without the slightest power of decision. For totalitarians, to express ideas contrary to their
slogans is already a crime.

The distinction drawn between so-called peaceful protestors—the
majority—and a small group of violent anarchists who, we are told, infil-
trate the former is misleading at best. Peacefully shutting down confer-
ences by physical means is obviously a contradiction in terms, and the
protestors' methods are identical to those perfected long ago by the black
and brown shirts and the Communist thugs. What's more, if violent
anarchists are really minorities in these devastating "raves," how does one
explain the inability of the peaceful majority to neutralize them? How is
it that one or two hundred thousand idealists enamored of peace are
impotent to contain a few hundred terrorists who have come to break,
wreck, burn, smash and pillage? Things could get out of hand once,
maybe, but six, seven, ten times? Far from diminishing between Seattle
in 1999 and Genoa in 2001, the violence winked at—or indulged in—
by the "peaceful" demonstrators has only grown more extreme.

In Genoa, when the Italian police stepped over the line in maintaining order and a twenty-year-old policeman killed a twenty-three-year-

old demonstrator, it was certainly a tragedy. But although the press and the political opposition furiously blamed the police and the government, the young man's death ought not to have been so controversial, for it was evident from pictures that the *carabiniere* was acting legitimately in self-defense.* In Göteborg, a town whose center had been "peacefully" demolished, the Swedish police had already cracked down on demonstrators using methods more appropriate for engaging guerrilla terrorists than mere demonstrators: they had opened fire using real bullets, causing injuries but fortunately no deaths. Though when it comes down to it, wasn't this really a case of urban guerrilla warfare? The ruse of these pseudo-demonstrators—actually, rioters—is to throw onto the police all responsibility for the violence that they themselves have initiated.

And so it has been for a long time. The ultra-right Paris rioters who were making for the Palais Bourbon (the seat of the French National Assembly) on February 6, 1934, with the intention of forcing entry and driving out the deputies—using exactly the same methods as today's agitators—blamed the police and only the police for the loss of life incurred when the latter answered force with force in defense of the Republic. Doubtless the gendarmes were not entirely innocent, but the rioters were less so. In both cases, police violence was the effect, not the cause, of the crowd's violence. Even before the opening ceremonies of the Genoa summit, police stations had received parcel bombs, and a public official who opened one of them lost an eye. Meanwhile, the peace-loving activists were already using precautionary Molotov cocktails in the city's streets.**

What is obvious from all this is that mayhem was sought for its own sake. For citizens of democratic countries, enjoying more or less full liberties, there is no rationale for such extremes: they have freedom of expression and the right to vote; and nothing prevents them from forming political parties (if they are so inclined) and running in elections where they can attempt to win support for their ideas through persuasion. So it seems a little odd that Prime Minister Jospin should compliment them for choosing a very different route.

It is against dictatorships that obstructionary tactics and violence are legitimate, because then they are the sole recourse for those striving to bring about democracy. But the rioters at Nice and Genoa did the

---

*See the article by D. Dunglas in *Le Point,* 27 July 2001.
***International Herald Tribune,* 18 July 2001.

opposite: they subverted democracy in order to replace it with a despotism of the mob.

■ ■ ■

TO UNDERSTAND THE ANTIGLOBALIZERS' mindset, it is useful to recall the old cultural cargo that they carry from the "revolutionary" tradition; you could say they are play-acting a revolution that has failed to manifest over the century or has fallen into disgrace. With incoherent ideas and a poverty of facts, they have no ambition to advance a program by democratic means, for the simple reason that they don't have such a program. Agitation comes before thought, perpetuating a premodern political history, much as certain Neolithic cults survived in subterranean fashion into the Renaissance. Relentlessly hammering on the archaic anticapitalist and anti-American drum, they chant mantras about the miraculous effectiveness of urban guerrilla warfare. And the opportunity to make a sacrifice of Silvio Berlusconi, president of the European Council, whom they regard as a "fascist" despite his having been democratically elected twice, added extra spice to their primitive rites.

The youthful antiglobalists are actually superannuated ideologues, revenants from a past of ruin and bloodshed. In Genoa we saw the reappearance of red flags adorned with hammer and sickle (which even the Italian ex-Communists had gotten rid of), effigies of Che Guevara and the acronym for the Red Brigades. America is the object of their loathing because, for a half-century or more, she has been the most prosperous and creative capitalist society on earth. Ultimately it is liberal democracy—or quite simply liberty itself—that they are eager to destroy, even though they are among its foremost beneficiaries, being free to travel anywhere, anytime in order to hatch their plots. If their *diktats* were carried out, if frontier barriers were reestablished everywhere, with passports and visas even for tourists, there could have been no Seattle and no Göteborg.

This is not the only contradiction in their impoverished mental bric-a-brac. For example, they brought mayhem to Seattle in the name of combating a "savage" globalization that "profits only the rich." Yet who were convening in Seattle? Representatives of the World Trade Organization (WTO), whose role is precisely to monitor international economic transactions and make them conform to rules—so as to prevent them from being "savage." Ever since its founding, there has not been a single country in the world that hasn't wanted to be admitted into the WTO, and the poorest are the most willing. At Nice and Göteborg were gathered representatives of the European Union, which, with fifteen member nations, can hardly be considered global (there are nearly two hundred nations worldwide). And Genoa saw a meeting of the G-8, that is, the seven most industrialized nations in the world, with the courtesy addition of Russia. Here again, although their influence obviously is international, they hardly constitute the entire world. They are not the United Nations. They may try to harmonize their policies, but any agreements have no binding force on other states.

Purporting to oppose globalism, the Genoa hooligans were really attacking capitalism (they had smashed the façades of banks even before the conference began) and its most diabolical manifestation: America. The pretext for this demonization was the old canting line of rich countries not caring enough for the poor countries of the world. In due course, I'll make a case for the inanity of this myth. But in the case of the G-8 summit it's interesting to note, furthermore, that its goal was specifically to deal with the issue of rich versus poor countries. The Eight effectively reduced the poorer nations' debt burden, stepping up aid targeted at development in the Southern Hemisphere and creating a global fund to finance the medical campaigns against AIDS, malaria and tuberculosis, especially in sub-Saharan Africa.

Moreover, at Genoa the G-8 members had for the first time invited African leaders to sit with them in open discussion. Prime Minister Tony Blair with good reason hailed the start of what he called "an ambitious Marshall Plan for Africa."* Even before the summit's opening, the dreadful George W. Bush had asked for "more loans for health and education in the poorest nations." He announced in this respect a "radical change of policy" by his administration, and he added, "But let's make no mistake: those who protest against free trade are no friends of the poor."** Though notoriously stupid in the eyes of the European press, the president was not altogether wrong. What the developing countries are asking for is freer access to the world's best markets for their products, especially agricultural products. In other words, they want *more* globalization, not less. So here is another aspect of the rioters' inconsistency:

---

*International Herald Tribune, 18 July 2001.
**International Herald Tribune, 23 July 2001.

well-heeled themselves, they are subverting summits whose goal is, by extending free trade, to strengthen poor countries' ability to export to the most solvent zones. Thus the 2001 Summit of the Americas at Quebec laid down the basis for a single continental market that would open North America to South American agricultural and other products—and once again the host city was invaded and wrecked.

If, in the hodgepodge of half-baked notions trumpeted in the activists' slogans, there is concealed some sort of program capable of practical application, I haven't been able to detect it. Instead, they display a useless farrago of hatreds, which makes it all the more astonishing when European leaders—not reputed to be nostalgic for paleosocialism—declare themselves "impressed" by the rioters and convinced of the necessity to "dialogue" with them. It is grotesque to see the leftist press and a whole political stratum that, since 1989, have grudgingly mumbled "heartbreaking reappraisals" of all the socialist catastrophes and absurdities now cry victory as they greet the divine surprise of this new crusade against globalism, synonymous of course with capitalism.

It is harder to understand why this antiglobalist muddle is taken seriously (at least in appearance) by leaders on the right of the political spectrum. Why did the president of the French Republic, Jacques Chirac, plead before his peers in favor of "normal and permanent dialogue" with the activists? Why did he proclaim that the time had come to "humanize globalization"?* So globalization is inhumane? Chirac's formula buys into the thugs' clichés and seconds the antidemocratic strategy of the recycled leftists and most of the NGOs. Following Jospin, Chirac even pays tribute to a "global social consciousness." Why the socialist jargon? It's true that this alignment is symptomatic of a peculiarly French syndrome of the Right. The other G-8 governments, even the social-democratic ones, haven't followed Chirac into this dead end. They have every intention of retaining the right to deliberate among themselves and with their fellow nations, without having to consult with totally illegitimate rioters. It's also true that, though France possesses a great tradition of liberal thinkers, the French political Right hasn't read them; it has always been and remains *dirigiste,* regulatory and bureaucratic. And the French Right, especially since the end of the Second World War, burns

---

Le Figaro, 10 July 2001.

with desire to please the Left—a passion all the more paralyzing because it is so unrequited.

Bernard Kouchner, whose aid programs for poor countries—*Médecins sans frontières* and *Médecins du monde*—command respect, nevertheless lost some of his lucidity when, after the riots against the G-8 in Genoa, he wrote: "It's May '68 on a worldwide scale!" No doubt about it, nothing claims to be more international than antiglobalism! Kouchner's pronouncement is amusing, but as history it isn't very enlightening; for the movement that we French like to call "May '68," on the pretext that it first broke out in France during this month, had actually begun several years before, in more original and less Marxist form, in the United States and later in Germany. In Europe, this movement, antitotalitarian in its origins, began idealistically or even beneficially with the agenda of transforming moral attitudes and lifestyles, but very soon pledged allegiance to the commonplaces of totalitarian socialism in its Maoist and Trotskyist versions. Refusing to play the game of democratic legality, and accepted for form's sake by the Western Communist parties, "May '68" degenerated over the course of the next twenty years into a sanguinary terrorism. So we saw the Red Brigades in Italy, the Baader-Meinhof Gang or Red Army Faction in Germany, the Japanese Red Army, the Belgian Fighting Communist Cells and, more marginal but no less murderous, Direct Action in France. We owe to these organizations deeds of valor that could not judiciously be offered as models to today's generation, who themselves are sometimes a hair's breadth from crossing the line into terrorism. The fatal step was actually taken when, in the name of anti-Americanism, a bomb was detonated in a McDonald's in Brittany, killing a young woman. This was in the spring of 2000.

There should be no surprise here. What the current crop of antiglobalizers have in common with the *soixante-huitards* is a simplistic Marxist article of faith: absolute evil is capitalism, incarnated in and directed by the United States. After Genoa there was much talk of organizing future but more modest G-8 summits; accordingly the humorist Plantu, in the July 24, 2001, issue of *Le Monde*, had a cartoon in which Uncle Sam—that guy again!—is seen camping in a tent whose pegs, planted in the ground, are the seven other members of G-8. Recognizable as one of the tent pegs is Jacques Chirac. The lesson is clear: the *real* master of G-8 is American capitalism, whose servants are the other democracies. Even *L'Humanité* around 1950 would never have run such a simple-minded caricature.

Common to the *soixante-huitards* of yesteryear and the antiglobal-izers of today is the brutal conviction that street demonstrators are more legitimate than elected governments. Here is one of the moldiest old rags hanging in the attic of Marxist dogma: the uprising of the "masses" is more democratic than "formal" democracy. Worse, eminent political fig-ures of the Left (in France, François Hollande, Jean-Luc Mélanchon, Noël Mamère, among others) demanded, after Genoa, the abolition of G-8. The conclusion to be drawn from this démarche: governments elected by democratic suffrage lose the right to take counsel together the moment that the street denies them this right.

It goes without saying that the size of a demonstration can indicate a significant trend in public opinion that democratic governments would be well advised to take into account, if only in anticipation of the next election. But they discredit themselves if they give in because demon-strators are violent to the point of paralyzing democracy itself; in such cases, democrats worthy of the name should not forget that power is con-ferred by ballots, not by bricks hurled through windows. It is disturbing that the Left too often ignores this principle.

The underlying idea is that anarchy is justified in the struggle against capitalist "arrogance"—an arrogance believed to be quintessentially Amer-ican. But it is curious nevertheless that whenever economic difficulties arise, and especially at times of crisis, it is first and foremost the United States that developing countries appeal to for aid or intervention. This is true alike for Asia, Africa, Latin America, Serbia and Russia.

On July 30, 2001, the president of the World Trade Organization warned that the slowness of negotiations and delays in implementing decisions concerning international trade were harming the world's poor-est countries. The main cause of these delays, he said, was the unwill-ingness of the advanced nations to reduce agricultural subsidies, an indirect form of protectionism. This economist, who is in a good position to observe the facts, was saying, in short, that the underlying cause of poverty is not the market economy but an insufficiently free market economy. Unsurprisingly, this verdict, however well supported by the data, would not move the leftists. Truth be told, they are indifferent to the fate of the underdeveloped countries; what they really want is to destroy the economies of the developed countries, inasmuch as development and capitalism are, in their eyes, one and the same. About this last point they are not mistaken.

. . .

THE REASON CURRENTLY INVOKED to condemn globalization is that it will accentuate inequalities and aggravate poverty. To judge the truth or falsity of this thesis—often accepted without critical examination even by defenders of the market economy—we should address three questions:

- Is market globalization bad in itself?
- Is it bad above all because, in its contemporary version, it offers a field for American power to expand into? And is humanity growing increasingly standardized as it becomes Americanized?
- Is it true that because of globalization the rich will become richer and the poor poorer, on the worldwide scale as well as within each country?

With regard to the first question, it's important to recall again that it is only *market* globalization that the Left rejects. In fact, the Left has always hoped for globalization, but *without* the market—in other words, an ideologically correct world government. Revolutionary France claimed the historical destiny to spread the principles of 1789 over the entire world; and socialism in the nineteenth and twentieth centuries defined itself as essentially internationalist, founding the First, Second, Third and Fourth Internationals, whose very names point to planet-wide ambitions. Despite transitory phases when, for tactical and economic reasons, consolidation and "socialism in one country" were the order of the day, the Soviet and Maoist Communists always felt the vocational urge to impose their models on the whole of humanity, if need be by military intervention or by armed subversion, which they did not hesitate to use on five continents.

Although they have neither the means nor even the intent to undertake bellicose operations on such a scale, today's antiglobalizers are not a jot less antiliberal and internationalist in their ambitions.* The leftist press, for example *Le Nouvel Observateur,* applauding the "success of the antiliberal summit of Porto Alegre," proclaimed—this is the article's title—the "Birth of an International." The conclusion: "Another globalization takes over from Davos." A clearer illustration of my contention is hard to imagine. Globalization is perfectly all right, provided that it's the planned and statist kind. The socialist prime minister, Lionel Jospin, after having applauded in Genoa, 2001, the *"worldwide* [my italics]

---

*See *L'Express,* 26 July 2001.

emergence of a socially aware movement," continued by compliment-
ing the demonstrators for having shown, according to him, that "control of globalization goes through the reaffirmation of states' roles." The
conflict therefore turns less on globalism itself than on opposing con-
ceptions of what kind it should be: one founded on free markets and private enterprise, the other on *dirigisme* and state-controlled economies, a
globalization imposed and controlled by concerted governments. If there
was a "victory,"* from Seattle to Genoa, it consisted in making the latter conception prevail.

The drawback of the *dirigiste* ambition, and the paradox of its resurgence and joyful reception nowadays, is that putting it into practice has
never in the past resulted in anything but disastrous economic decline,
poverty or even destitution of the people and pronounced technological
backwardness, accompanied more often than not by political tyranny.
This assessment is as valid for Communist-socialist states as for Hitle-
rian National Socialism, which (let's not forget) also conceived of itself
as destined to dominate the entire world, Europe for starters. Just so,
dirigiste globalism has always been an instigator of human catastrophes,
or at the very least of economic collapses far more grievous in their effect
on the people than the worst capitalist injustices.

Historical and present reality shows that only capitalism can deliver
a form of globalism whose balance sheet, while not entirely without lia-
bilities, is on the whole positive; and it has a long history.

Globalism existed long before the birth of the United States. As the
economist and historian Régis Bénichi reminds us in a lucid overview
of the subject, it has accompanied the entire history of capitalism.**
Already in Roman times and during the Middle Ages, the beneficial
effects of widening commerce were evident: the advantages of reciproc-
ity and complementarity resulted in lower costs for goods. But it was not
until after the great explorations at the end of the fifteenth century and
the growth of transatlantic trade that globalization in the modern sense
of the term began. Bénichi identifies three waves: the development of
merchant capitalism after the discoveries; the spread of the industrial

---

*This is Jean Daniel's choice of words, in "Gênes, le sens d'une victoire," *Le Nouvel
Observateur,* 21 July 2001.
**Régis Bénichi, "La mondialisation aussi a une histoire," *L'Histoire,* no. 254, May
2001. *Le Figaro,* 24 July 2001.

revolution in Europe and North America; and finally the process we are witnessing today.

The first wave began during the sixteenth century and grew in strength during the seventeenth. Thanks to maritime commerce, not only the leading players in this drama like England and Spain, but small countries like Portugal and Holland became great economic powers at the center of worldwide networks extending to India, Southeast Asia, Indonesia, the western Pacific, Australia and southern Africa. The Dutch East India Company was a prototype for the new engines of global commerce.* The eighteenth century saw the implementing of free trade as well as greater theoretical understanding of its benefits.

In the course of what Bénichi calls the second wave of globalization, from about 1840 to 1914, the volume of commerce increased sevenfold. There is much talk nowadays of an "American world," but it was Europe that created the first two world markets, as her capital, technologies, languages and people spread over every continent; she was the driving force of an international circulation of commodities, scientific knowledge, ideas and techniques. But after the catastrophe of the First World War, Europe drew back and turned in on herself. Her supremacy was a thing of the past. Moreover, she became divided within as countries erected barriers against each other. On the other side of the Atlantic, the United States, Argentina and Brazil, whose immense territories were traditionally open to immigrants and foreign products, barricaded themselves in their turn. International trade plummeted, capital could no longer circulate, exchange controls were instituted and there were efforts to fix currencies by decree. Thus, all over the world, economic life stagnated and came to resemble what today's enemies of globalism desire for us. The result was not long in coming: the stock market crash of 1929, followed by the Great Depression, which lasted a decade with tens of millions unemployed, and the rise of dictatorships and totalitarian regimes as a consequence of the universal and precipitous decline in living standards. (France, for example, would not return to her 1914 average per capita income level until the beginning of the 1950s.) And to crown this brilliant series of successes came the Second World War, from which Europe emerged not only materially and economically destroyed, but this time deposed for good from great-power status.

---

*On the subject of Dutch economic power in the eighteenth century, see Simon Schama's masterly study *The Embarrassment of Riches* (New York: Knopf, 1987).

So whatever the demonstrators of Genoa or Davos think about the matter, it is understandable that in 1945 the "international community," as it was later called, should for once have drawn lessons from its mistakes and dared to turn its back on the antiglobalism of the previous quarter-century. As early as 1941, in mid-war, the United States had written the freeing of world commerce into the Atlantic Charter, signed on August 14 by Churchill and Roosevelt. And in 1944, Henry Morgenthau, Roosevelt's secretary of the treasury, announced the doctrine that was to serve as a guideline for the future:

> What are the fundamental conditions under which the commerce among nations can once more flourish?
>
> First, there must be a reasonable, stable standard of international exchange to which all countries can adhere without sacrificing the freedom of action necessary to meet their internal economic problems.
>
> This is the alternative to the desperate tactics of the past—competitive currency depreciation, excessive tariff barriers, uneconomic barter deals, multiple practices, and unnecessary exchange restrictions—by which governments vainly sought to maintain employment and uphold living standards. In the final analysis, these tactics only succeeded in contributing to worldwide depression and even war. The International Monetary Fund agreed upon at Bretton Woods will help remedy this situation.*

Thus began the third wave of globalization, which has continued since the end of the Second World War. After the fall of Communism, the capitalist features of this third phase are increasingly evident. Inevitably it is colored by America's emergence as sole superpower, and it should not be surprising therefore if it has an even more capitalistic character than the earlier phases, which is to say it owes increasingly more to private enterprise and less and less to the undertakings of states. For, even in nations where *political* Communism has tried artificially to prolong its existence, surviving Communist governments have made every effort to get rid of economic socialism by means of privatization, appeals to foreign investors, deregulation of commerce and establishment of cross-border trade agreements. Only Cuba and North Korea have clung to totalitarian collectivism—no comment necessary here.

---

*From the closing address by U.S. Secretary of the Treasury Henry Morgenthau, 22 July 1944, at the Bretton Woods Conference.

■ ■ ■

SO IF ECONOMIES AT THE END of the twentieth and beginning of the twenty-first century should be at once globalized, capitalist and dominated by the Americans, it has nothing to do with any sort of "arrogance." It is not even the result of choice. It flows from a historically determined conjunction of three sets of indisputable facts.

First: the economic and political cataclysms that were brought about by the closed economies of Europe between the World Wars. Second: the ample and definitive demonstration of socialism's incapacity to deliver the economic goods, even minimally. Third: the self-caused enfeebling of the Europeans' position in the world—they alone are responsible for their own heaped-up aberrations and follies over the first half of the century. This weakening entailed the corresponding and virtually automatic rise of the United States.

Nevertheless, the Americans' ascendancy is not just a relative phenomenon attributable to the demotion of Europe; it also stems from intrinsic factors peculiar to their society. Strikingly, moreover, they continue to increase their lead in spite of the European economic recovery since the Second World War, even since the consolidation of the European Union. A united Europe should in theory be up to the task of acting as a counterbalance to the United States. And if it hasn't yet risen to the challenge, this is obviously not for lack of material and human resources, but for lack of understanding of how to use them. Europe hasn't shown nearly enough inventiveness, organizational talent and adaptive flexibility. Inhibited by ideological prejudices, Europe, despite its successes, continues to live overshadowed by America. Witness the fact that the health of her economy is dependent on the state of America's economy: when the latter goes into recession, as in the beginning of 2001, Europe falters.

Is globalism to be deemed poisonous merely by virtue of its association with Americanization? Must we close our eyes to the achievements of the years between 1948 and 1998, when worldwide production grew by a factor of six and the volume of exports by seventeen? Must direct investment abroad, the engine of progress for the less-developed countries, be proscribed just because it is, for the most part, American investment? Let me say again: what the developing countries need is *more* globalization, for as yet the latter remains very uneven, with the greater part of trade and investment occurring between the nations of the European Union, North America and the Asia-Pacific region.

No matter how much the antiglobalizers destroy in Seattle or Nice, it's hard to see what they would replace their bugbear with. Or perhaps they would like to return to the sort of Third World socialism that, in a few decades, reduced the African continent from semipoverty to complete destitution.

As for the fear that every country has of seeing its "identity" melted down in American standardization, and Europe's struggle to preserve its "cultural diversity," these are difficult to analyze exactly, so disparate are the complaints. All mixed up are worries about preserving languages against the universalizing juggernaut of English, disapproval of McDonald's hamburgers and young people's fondness for Levis, fears about the impact of Hollywood and American made-for-TV movies, and resentment over American universities' scientific fecundity. But underlying all these emotions is the same obsession, above all among the Europeans, that ends up imputing to a calculated "imperialism" what actually results from a convergence of various historical trends, the most important of which often flow from the mistakes of the presumed victims of this imperialism.

Hubert Védrine, a close collaborator of and diplomatic advisor to President François Mitterrand over fourteen years, spokesman and then general secretary to the presidency of the Republic, finally minister of foreign affairs for Jospin's government from 1997 to 2002, wrote in his book *Les Mondes de François Mitterrand:* "The foremost characteristic of the United States, which explains its foreign policy, is that it has regarded itself ever since its birth as a chosen nation, charged with the task of enlightening the rest of the world."

What is immediately striking about this pronouncement, the obvious fact that jumps right out, is how perfectly it applies to France herself. Even the American quotations that Védrine produces in support of his thesis nearly all have their literal equivalents in the clichés of French political and cultural narcissism. When he chides Thomas Jefferson for saying that "the United States is the empire of liberty"—a "peremptory affirmation," according to Védrine—how could we not think of the slogan, no less peremptory, that is trotted out every day in our press and by our politicians: "France is the birthplace of the Rights of Man"? And when the former diplomatic advisor to François Mitterrand denounces the "hegemonic notion" he detects in Ezra Hiles's declaration, around 1800, that "Ships will carry the American flag all around the world," anyone in France who knows history will recall Lamartine's flamboyant and celebrated remark at the time of the 1848 Revolution, when the poet-turned-politician saluted the "tricolored flag [that] has gone around the world."* Finally, it would be easy to multiply quotations from General de Gaulle depicting the "whole world, which has its gaze fixed on France."

These megalomaniac hypotheses, which have so often made us look ridiculous, do not belong only to the past. In July 2001, Lionel Jospin broached the issue of globalization when he addressed the personnel of the "French Cultural Cooperation Network" gathered at the Ministry of Foreign Affairs. "From now on," he told them, "you will be a public network of influence and solidarity on a worldwide scale, our own decisive trump card in the high-stakes challenge of globalization confronting our country."** Beneath the apparent illogicality of these words (to fight against globalization on the one hand, to act by means of it on the other) there lies a coherent thought, namely, that it is liberal, American-style globalization that we must thwart with *our* brand of globalization, which Jospin went on to say would work towards the "affirmation of states against the unbridled laws of the market." That a country should feel itself possessed of a universal vocation and proclaim as much is not in itself reprehensible; but when that country happens to be the United States and not France—that's what must be condemned. Therefore, France must replace America as the global leader.

This is the lesson that Hubert Védrine likewise draws from his assessment of the situation at the same meeting, with an optimistic prognosis: "Now that the threat of an excessive homogenization is looming, France again has a good hand to play." As it happened, the minister of foreign affairs had some months earlier added to the list of his published books

---

*It's worth recalling the exact quotation. On 24 February 1848, at the Hôtel de Ville, addressing the socialists who wanted to adopt the red flag as emblem of the Second Republic, Lamartine rejoined: "The red flag you're bringing back has never gone further than a turn around the Champ de Mars, dragged in the people's blood in '91 and '93, but the tricolored flag has gone all around the world, bearing the name, the glory and the liberty of the country." However moving, this mythopoetic flight manifests conviction in a "globalist" legitimacy—France as supreme guide for other nations.

**Le Monde, 25 July 2001.

one entitled *Les Cartes de la France* ("France's Hand of Cards"). There he develops, like Jospin, the idea that the threat of the American hyperpower has given new impetus to France's own vocation and universalist mission, which is to promote its own form of globalism in opposition to America's.

But the notion that a worldwide intermingling of economies and cultures would be destructive is false. Consider the powerful influence of Greece in antiquity, Italy in the sixteenth century, France in the eighteenth, Britain in the nineteenth: not one of these annihilated the cultures it dominated; on the contrary, the distinctive characteristics of the latter were often strengthened.

Let me clarify: it is indisputable that the overarching preponderance of the United States has presented other countries with new problems in many domains—and the cultural domain is not the least important, a subject I'll come back to. But this primacy is the product of historical processes spanning nearly a century. It is well to analyze these currents in order to face the present situation rationally, so that we can capitalize on what is positive and correct excesses that threaten international equilibrium. But the resentment that leads to the rejection of every idea that comes from America simply because it is American can only weaken countries that take their phobias as guiding principles. Such an irrational aversion limits a country's ability to deal with the world and elicits contempt in many countries that are far from being predictably pro-American.

Reflecting on the reasons for the drubbing Paris received when she submitted her candidacy to host the 2008 Olympics, Jacques Julliard wrote with perceptiveness and candor:

> In Moscow we have been abandoned by our European partners, by our Arab "friends" and by our African supporters. The plain, unvarnished truth—which the whole political community does everything it can to hide—is that France has become one of the least popular countries on the planet. I have already mentioned its arrogance and vanity. To these should be added the way our rulers presume to lecture the entire world.*

"The entire world" is perhaps not the most accurate phrase. We don't lecture Saddam Hussein, Muammar al-Qaddafi, Kim Jong Il, Fidel Castro,

---

*Jacques Julliard, "Sur une déculottée," *Le Nouvel Observateur,* 19 July 2001. The meeting of the International Olympic Committee before choosing the host city for the 2008 Olympics took place in Moscow.

Robert Mugabe, the imams of the Islamic Republic of Iran or the bosses of China and Vietnam. We reserve our admonitions and our contempt for the democracies: Austria, Italy, Margaret Thatcher, Ronald Reagan, George W. Bush, Silvio Berlusconi and even, because he is insufficiently hostile to capitalism, Tony Blair. The enemy is not the dictators but the market economy.

■ ■ ■

Nor is the enemy poverty, whatever the slogans claim. What's important to the antiglobalizers is not the eradication of poverty; rather, it is the propaganda value they gain from linking poverty to liberalism and the spreading market economy.

If there's one axiom universally held to be true, by defenders and opponents of the world market alike, it is that the gap between rich and poor is widening, or as the canard goes, that the poor are getting poorer and the rich, richer.

To begin with, note that these two statements are not equivalent. The income gap can widen between societies, or between individuals within a society, even while the living standard of the poor rises. If a developed industrial society sees its per capita annual income rise in ten years from $20,000 to $30,000—that is, by one-third—and if over the same period a less advanced country sees a proportionally equal per capita rise from $3,000 to $4,500, the gap between the two countries will have increased: from $17,000 per annum to $25,500. The inequality has grown, but the standard of living in the poorer society has nonetheless been raised, a fact that will be greatly appreciated by its members.

There is abundant and sound documentation, extending back over fifty years, that the countries formerly called "Third World" have experienced increases in average income, in population and in life expectancy. The last has more than doubled over the second half of the twentieth century. In India, for example, food production grew by a factor of ten, leading to the elimination of the massive famines that used to be so frequent. This is not enough to prevent a large part of the Indian population (which has quadrupled over the same period of time) from living at an unacceptably low standard; but, contrary to popular clichés, the standard of living continues to rise. And in any case, the best way to ensure that it keeps climbing is certainly not to strangle the global marketplace. In Latin America, from 1950 to 1985, real per capita income in constant dollars (valued at the 1975 level) doubled, going from about $1,000 per annum to a little over $2,000, which was Western Europe's level circa 1950. Mexico in 1985 is higher on the scale in terms of per capita income than was Italy in 1960. During the past five decades, Latin America on the whole has experienced an annual growth of 5 percent. No European country can boast an equivalent sustained average growth rate.

These figures show to what an extent the mantras about ever-increasing poverty spring from ignorance or pure dishonesty. Continuing poverty, regular bankruptcies of public finances, inflation and the flight of capital are not the result of an intractable underdevelopment per se, but of incompetence and corruption, the wasting of international aid and the persistence of a ruinously inefficient public sector.

This regrettable state of affairs is most obvious in the case of Africa, the only Third World continent to have witnessed a decline, not just relative to the wealthy nations, but in real and absolute terms. This impoverishment has political, not economic, causes. It is statism rather than the market, and socialism rather than capitalism that have seriously harmed or destroyed the African economies. After independence, the African elites who formed the political leadership for the most part adopted the Soviet and Chinese systems. Through this means they were able to assume absolute power with access to the levers of personal enrichment. And from Communism they borrowed an infallible recipe for agricultural ruin: from Algeria to Tanzania they collectivized the land, setting up "cooperatives" that quickly became unproductive. I will not elaborate here on this subject, which I have dealt with at length in several books and which has been analyzed exhaustively by scholars with more expertise on the topic.* Such disquisitions, alas, have been to no effect, since the Third World's false friends have no intention of seeing that the world's poor have enough to eat, their enthusiasm being focused rather on blaming capitalism for the impoverishment that is socialism's offspring.

On top of the African nomenklaturas' deadly borrowings from Sino-Soviet kolkhozes (collective farms) and the local oligarchies' shameless

---

*Numerous articles on this subject can be found in my collection *Fin du siècle des ombres* (Fayard, 1999). But all my previous books, from *Without Marx or Jesus* (1970) to *Regain démocratique* (1992), with *The Totalitarian Temptation* (1976) in between, include chapters dealing with the question.

pillaging of internal resources and foreign aid, there are the incessant civil or interstate wars, religious wars, tribal feuds, massacres and genocides that are the principal if not the only explanation for Africa's free-fall into poverty. The civil wars that have starved and exterminated millions of people in the "Democratic" Republic of the Congo since 1997 are an outstanding example, but not the only one nor the last, I'm afraid. Several thousand copies of the Polish author Ryszard Kapuscinski's masterpiece, *The Shadow of the Sun,* a magnificently moving description of Africa's misery that also diagnoses its causes, should be distributed to the antiglobalist protestors.* Kapuscinski has for years traveled the length and breadth of the continent. But the privileged pseudo-revolutionaries of Seattle and Göteborg are careful to avoid any understanding of the real causes of the African cataclysm and careless about finding remedies; they prefer to hurl brickbats at their perennial hobgoblin.

One of their favorite canticles calls for the ritual "cancellation of Third World debt." The Pope conducts the choir and political groupings of every stripe intone the refrain. Now, debt implies money loaned to the borrower, and clearly one cannot repay what one has not previously received; so what has become of the sums accepted as loans, not to speak of the gifts pure and simple? In Madagascar, for instance, what did Didier Ratsiraka do with the billions of francs he received, a fortune that the starving Madagascan people never had the slightest whiff of? In 1990 François Mitterrand canceled the debt, saddling the French taxpayers with the burden of the thieving dictator's pocket money.

An investigative journalist could do well to search for traces in Switzerland or elsewhere of the billions of dollars stolen by the Nigerian dictator Sani Abacha, who died (or was assassinated?) in 1998. And what's the point of canceling the debt of Robert Mugabe, a typical president-dictator who has rigged every election in Zimbabwe and has managed in twenty years to transform one of the most fertile lands of Africa into one of the most unproductive?

Another chant from the antiliberal hymnal is the urgent need for a "Marshall Plan for Africa." The refrain is repeated ad nauseam—with relentless avoidance, it's apparent, of one annoying little detail: there have been several Marshall Plans for Africa, stretching back forty years, all without result. You could even say that Africa has been the beneficiary

---

* *The Shadow of the Sun* (Knopf, 2001).

of a sort of Permanent Marshall Plan:* Between 1960 and 2000 she received *four times* as much funding and aid per capita (never reimbursed, naturally) as Latin America or Asia. How was it that these last two took off economically, and not Africa?

What the antiliberals refuse to accept is that, on the one hand, the so-called less-advanced peoples are on the whole advancing, and on the other, those who are faltering owe their misfortunes to internal political scourges and not to the world market economy. But it is pointless to argue against bad faith; attempts to set forth the facts are greeted with gales of righteous indignation.

Thus, in 2000 the economist Albert Merlin evoked caustic rejoinders with an article in *Les Échos* summarizing and commenting on a report by the World Bank that, with the exception of *The Economist,* was totally ignored. And with reason! The work of two respected economists, David Dollar and Aart Krav, the report demolishes the dogma that globalization leads to pauperization. Dollar and Krav prove the contrary, thanks to a meticulous survey of 125 countries over a period of forty years. According to their detailed facts and figures, income in the poorest countries—those in the lowest quintile on the scale—has grown at the same rate, over the long haul, as in the rest of the world taken as a whole. And the benefits of accelerated general growth during the last five years of the twentieth century have not diminished. So free trade and the market economy have a positive effect overall: when the world's average per capita income rises by 1 percent, incomes in the poorest countries rise by the same proportion in accordance with what Dollar and Krav have dubbed the "one-to-one law." Albert Merlin sums up: "This argument is sufficient (or should be sufficient) to demolish the current theses about growing poverty and the horrors of free trade."

It may be objected that economists are often wrong. This is undeniable, but it is when they try to *forecast* that economists are most often wrong. The World Bank's report makes no attempt to forecast; it is descriptive and firmly anchored in historical facts.

If anyone was completely wrong in his predictions, it was René Dumont, the "father of French ecology" and of Third Worldism, whose death in July 2001 was marked by adulatory obituaries. In numerous articles devoted to his writings and activism, he was highly praised for having

---

*The phrase is from Yves Plattard, who was French ambassador to several African countries.

"foreseen" around 1960 that worldwide food production could not keep pace with demographic growth. Dumont's prediction was hardly original; it was a rehashing of the old theory expounded in 1798 by Malthus in his *Essay on the Principle of Population*. Already shown to be erroneous in Malthus's case, this notion was ridiculed in Dumont's. The "World Report on Human Development" (2001) shows that average per capita daily calorie intake grew by about one-quarter between 1970 and 1997, although populations doubled or tripled in the majority of countries. The exception to the rule is Africa, for reasons that I have already stated, unrelated to economics.

In the art of manipulating poorly understood terms, or terms whose meanings are never explained, the expression "poverty line" occupies an honored place. There is hardly a newspaper, radio or television piece relating to the developing nations that doesn't drum in the idea that the population of such-and-such a country, or of the entire world, is "living below the poverty line." But never is this notorious line scientifically defined.

The poverty line is calculated not from the average income, but from the *median* income of each country. A line is drawn bisecting the lower half of the income scale, below the median, and any household whose income level is situated in the lowest quarter is considered poor. Obviously, the "poor" in very rich countries, where median incomes are high, enjoy very different standards of living from the poor of countries that are themselves mired in poverty. A "poor" person in Sweden would be a nabob in Nepal. But we don't need to go so far as the Himalayas or to the least developed countries. A poor American (earning $8,000 annually as a single individual) enjoys an income approximately equal to the *average* in Greece or Portugal, which is considered an altogether adequate and comfortable level in those countries. And the poor American's income is actually higher, since, falling "below the poverty line," he automatically becomes eligible for benefits flowing from a variety of social programs. Many are the misleading statements made in the name of the poverty-line formulation, which is as pervasive as it is nebulous.

In spreading the lie that globalization impoverishes the most needy, the socially concerned protestors act upon twin enthusiasms: on the one hand, the anti-American obsession, which goes back to the Cold War and further into the past; on the other, the habitual antiliberalism of the Left. A floating mass of some hundreds of thousands of demonstrators is thus compensating for the frustration of having seen all the socialisms and all the revolutions fail. "Revolutionaries without a revolution," they are devoid of an intelligible program to replace globalism. Their rhetoric cannot even boast the spurious coherence of yesteryear's totalitarian ideologies. By yelling slogans, they afford themselves the illusion of thought; by trashing cities and striving to stymie international gatherings, they provide themselves with the illusion of action.

Hatred for liberal civilization is for many, then, the key to the anti-American obsession, and it goes far back into the past. Hubert Beuve-Méry, the future founder and editor of *Le Monde,* wrote in May 1944:

> The Americans constitute a real danger for France—a danger different in kind from the threat represented by Germany, and the threat that may eventually emerge from Russia. . . . The Americans can always prevent us from making the necessary revolution and their materialism does not even have the tragic grandeur of the materialism of the totalitarians. If they cling to a veritable cult of the idea of liberty, they don't feel the need to liberate themselves from the servitudes that their capitalism entails.*

For such an opinion to be expressed at a moment when the Allied landings to come might still have failed, when Nazi power, although weakened, still held Europe in subjugation, and when the truth about Stalinism was known, there had to be a hierarchy of values and dangers that demonized liberalism as a threat to be feared above all others.

Réflexions politiques, 1932-1952 (Éditions *Le Monde* and Seuil, 1951).

3. Hatreds and Fallacies

IT COULD BE SAID THAT America itself is not problematic. The real issue is her relations with the rest of the world—relations both practical and moral—as well as problems that are often purely imaginary.

What I mean is: it isn't difficult to get to know the United States as she really is, with her virtues and her faults, both as a society and as an externally projected superpower. There is a vast wealth of reliable material dealing with America's many faces and underlying realities; for the curious, books and articles packed with information and insights are coming out all the time and in many languages. Scholarly studies on social and cultural life abound, as does original and well-documented reportage; American journalists, if they did not invent the genre of investigative reporting, have conspicuously been its leading exponents. So whoever wishes to be educated on the United States has every means of doing so, even without going there. And given the available resources, whoever remains poorly informed, even after frequent visits to the U.S., must simply want to be so. The question is, why?

You might answer that human beings generally have better things to do than pass their days absorbing libraries of books and thick sheaves of press clippings; or that, in those still too numerous countries where illiteracy predominates, such a task is impossible. Of course. But it ought to be the responsibility of opinion makers to act as reliable intermediaries between the public and the sources that they, as professionals, have the time and duty to be familiar with. It is up to them to share this knowledge in digestible form. Journalists are both historians of the present and educators. If they use their forums narcissistically to trumpet their own preconceived ideas instead of serving facts, they are betraying their public.

Because the United States is *the* geostrategic superpower, and in many respects a crucible of social and cultural patterns imitated throughout the world, it is vital that we get to know her—especially if we count ourselves among those who would like to see her influence reduced. For this can be achieved only by meeting the Americans with pertinent counter-proposals based on realistic policies. But spinning out prejudice-inspired resentments is futile, and the likely result is powerlessness.

No society is fault-free, of course. America has made her share of foreign policy mistakes. What country hasn't? Because of America's commanding position in the world, these mistakes can be all the more disastrous; so exposing them is vital—provided they are real mistakes. Meanwhile, critics should never lose sight of America's achievements. The goal is truth and impartiality, not the stroking of egos by those who indulge in fantasies of revenge. But in the realm of real-world policy, such dream-world analysis serves only to weaken the critics' positions still more.

Take, for example, the way that after September 11, the belief spread and was quickly accepted as factual that the U.S. government was bent on imposing censorship. What was this all about?

Al-Jazeera, the Qatar-based television channel, and subsequently CNN had aired a statement by Osama bin Laden in which he gloated over the thousands killed and called for further massacres. According to both American and French experts on terrorism, this tirade may have contained coded messages to "sleepers" in the United States or in Europe about projected terrorist attacks. It therefore seemed prudent for the U.S. administration and Congress to appeal to television and radio managers not to broadcast such communiqués, or at least to show caution and good judgment before airing them. Obviously, any government that refrained from taking such a commonsense step could be accused of criminal negligence; and for this reason the Department of State enjoined Voice of America not to broadcast an interview with Mullah Omar, the terrorist chief and close advisor to bin Laden.

As for monitoring the Internet, this is amply explained by the discovery—too late, alas—that the hijackers who destroyed the World Trade Center had been able to send numerous e-mails to each other, confident of evading detection. Everywhere, we heard it said that if the FBI and the CIA, whose failures were rightly being shouted from the rooftops, had kept a more vigilant eye on the Internet, they might have been alert to the suspect nature of some of the messages and placed their senders and receivers under observation.

Such precautionary measures ought to have been understood as legitimate steps, given the thousands of Americans murdered and the trauma experienced by everyone. Instead, a chorus of imprecations was raised up around the world. America had imposed censorship, suppressed freedom of the press, violated the First Amendment. "PROPAGANDA RAGES IN THE AMERICAN MEDIA,"* which had become "ITS MASTER'S VOICE"**—these are typical of the fevered headlines.

The legions of Muslims living in countries that have never known democracy or the slightest whiff of press freedom are apparently well qualified to defend these goods against the only country on the planet where they have never been suppressed. As for the French (to confine ourselves to one European country and to the relatively recent past), they have evidently already forgotten how, when the Algerian War was being fought, radio and television were subject to vigilant censorship by the state and scarcely a week went by without a police raid on some newspaper office or other to seize printed material that might "undermine the army's morale." And the calumniators fail to mention the American press's perpetual nervousness about threats to their First Amendment rights, especially the threats posed by a state of war.[†]

Other measures adopted after September 11 to thwart terrorist attacks (similar to those taken in Europe, by the way) raised protests on both sides of the Atlantic. Surveillance of suspects, access to e-mail and bank accounts, giving police the right to open car trunks—these precautions were denounced as "totalitarian" by some American civil liberties organizations as well as by the French League of Human Rights. Yet the measures were designed precisely to protect democracy from its totalitarian enemies. Worse, civil liberties groups in the United States have succeeded for some years now in preventing the passage of a law authorizing police agencies and intelligence services to implement such preventive measures;

---

*Title of an article in *Le Monde*, 3 October 2001.
**Title of an editorial by Tariq Zemmouri in *Jeune Afrique-l'intelligent*, 16 October 2001.
†See, for example, Marvin Kalb, "When the Press Is Asked, What Side Are You On?" *International Herald Tribune*, 12 October 2001; originally printed in the *Washington Post*. Also James Poniewozik, "The Battle for Hearts and Minds," *Time*, 22 October 2001.

had they been in force at an earlier date, the disasters in New York and Washington might well have been averted.

There is little point in deriding, however justly, the FBI and the CIA when it is demonstrated after the event that they could fairly easily have identified and preemptively neutralized the kamikaze pilots—since at the same time, the legislature has refused to grant the necessary special powers. But this is exactly what happened. After the 1998 terrorist attacks against U.S. embassies in Africa, Congress set up a National Commission on Terrorism (NCT) responsible for preparing a bill redefining antiterrorist policy. The commission emphasized in its report that the U.S. government did not yet have the means to anticipate and forestall al-Qaᶜida's attacks even on American soil, and that "the threat of attacks causing massive loss of human life within our borders continues to grow." On the report's cover was a photo of the Twin Towers—as if by premonition. Predictably, a swarm of leagues, associations and organizations leapt to the defense of what they imagined were "mortally endangered" liberties. An organization representing Arab-Americans bewailed a "return to the darkest days of McCarthyism." The civil rights chief in the Clinton administration criticized the NCT, charging that its report unjustly fingered Americans of Arab origin. But there is not a single mention of Arab-Americans in the commission's report! For others, the NCT's conclusions were obviously manufactured to satisfy the frustrated hawks who, deprived of an enemy since the end of the Cold War, found in terrorism a made-to-measure foe. All in all, the campaign was so noisy that the bill was effectively buried, never to become law—with results we all know.*

Although this was the most spectacular, it was far from being the only example of a clear-sighted American analysis that foresaw the emergence of a new kind of terrorist warfare on home territory. The fact that the defenders of human rights wouldn't take into account the right to national defense, which goes in tandem with the defense of liberty, and that they managed to dismiss these sensible warnings as the racist ravings of defense-obsessed fanatics only goes to show once again the naïve blindness of democratic regimes. As long as calamity isn't actually crashing down on them, democracies are careful to maintain their vulnerabil-

---

*There is a comprehensive account of this scandal in Franklin Foer's "Sin of Commission: How an Anti-Terrorist Report Got Ignored," *New Republic*, 8 October 2001.

ity. But in no way does this ingenious propensity for suicide entitle Europeans to brandish slogans denouncing a supposed erosion of American liberties—as if the danger of "fascism" were particularly severe in the U.S.A., a land that in over two hundred years has never known a dictator, while Europe has been busy making troops of them.

The main reproof that might be leveled at the American "hyperpower" is that it has deranged the minds of the rest of humanity—inducing in some a thirst for revenge, and in others, apparently, an incapacity for detached and lucid analysis.

■ ■ ■

THUS THE AMERICANS' military operation in Afghanistan, their first major undertaking after September 11, was quickly written up as a specimen of aggressive unilateralism. Washington, in a spasm of fright, had acted preemptively—as if no prior event could explain this "imperialistic" reflex.

African responses to America's actions were almost unanimous and entirely predictable. Also not surprising was the reaction of Latin America, where anti-Americanism is organically linked to the subcontinent's history, serving as a fantasy compensation for South America's failure relative to the North. As the great Venezuelan writer Carlos Rangel put it:

> For Latin Americans, it is an unbearable thought that a handful of Anglo-Saxons, arriving much later than the Spanish and in such a harsh climate that they barely survived the first few winters, would become the foremost power in the world. It would require an inconceivable effort of collective self-analysis for Latin Americans to face up to the fundamental causes of this disparity. This is why, though aware of the falsity of what they are saying, every Latin American politician and intellectual must repeat that all our troubles stem from North American imperialism.*

One would hope for a more nuanced reaction from Europe, where anti-Americanism, in spite of everything, is less automatic and less virulent than in Africa or Latin America—rooted as it is in a less pronounced

---

*Carlos Rangel, *Du bon sauvage au bon révolutionnaire* (Robert Laffont, 1976), translated from the Spanish, *Del buen salvaje al buen revolucionario* (Monte Avila, 1976). There is an English edition, *The Latin Americans: Their Love-Hate Relationship with the United States*, trans. Ivan Kats, with a foreword by Jean-François Revel (Harcourt Brace Jovanovich, 1977).

failure. And it's true that in the European Union, governments and public opinion generally showed unqualified solidarity with the United States
for the injustice she had suffered on September 11. Nevertheless, important minorities—in the old and the new parties of the Left, the Greens
in particular, and a near-majority among intellectuals and the enemies
of globalization—were quick to exhibit their old fixations. According to
them, hostilities really began only with the American retaliation; the whole
introductory act of the drama was scratched out, as it had been in the case
of the Gulf War by large numbers of people for whom the initial aggression, the war's absolute cause, was the twenty-eight-country coalition's
offensive on January 16, 1991, to drive the Iraqi army out of Kuwait.
Dropped from memory was Iraq's invasion nearly six months earlier.

Such curious chronological distortions prompted 113 French intellectuals to launch an appeal against the "imperial crusade" in Afghanistan.
"This is not our war," they proclaimed. "In the name of the law and
morality of the jungle [and not because three thousand people had been
assassinated], the Western armada [sic] administers its divine justice."
Why divine? If any parties in this entire affair believed themselves to be
divinely inspired, it was the Islamists—the kind that murders thousands
of innocent civilians in the name of Allah, or the kind that, in Nigeria
and Sudan, massacres Christians for being unwilling to submit to the
sharia. In September and October of 2001 alone, several hundred Nigerian Christians were exterminated by Muslims and our 113 intellectuals
had nothing to say about it. Yes, President Bush did use the word "crusade" when speaking of the necessary international mobilization against
terrorism. But for anyone of good faith who heard him, it was obvious
that what he meant was a campaign waged by a union of democracies,
not a "holy war." And holy war, of course, is the specialty of the Islamists,
as they never cease to proclaim.

As much should be obvious to everyone—except, of course, to the
113 intellectuals. Once again they have caused roles to be reversed, attribut-
ing to the democracies the whole gamut of "inspired," megalomaniac,
frenzied and homicidal tendencies that characterize Islamo-terrorism.

In the best of cases, and with commendable indulgence, the Amer-
icanophobes put the jihadists and those who would resist them on an
equal plane, not pronouncing in favor of either. So hundreds of thousands of pacifists, in the United States and in Europe (notably in Italy),

demonstrated on October 14, 2001, brandishing banners that said: "NO TO TERRORISM. NO TO WAR." Which is about as intelligent as: "NO TO ILLNESS. NO TO MEDICINE."

Marco Pannella, the charismatic founding president of the Italian Radical Party, put it this way: "We are well aware, since 1938, who is the supreme enemy that must, in the name of peace, be combated. At that time the pacifists launched a sacred struggle against the demo-judeo-plutocracies of London, Paris and New York."* In 1939, after the German-Soviet Nonaggression Pact, when the Nazi armies were only weeks from occupying Paris, French Communists, fixated on capitalism, exhorted armaments workers to sabotage their factories and soldiers to desert their regiments. But, continued Pannella, "An imperialist war had to be opposed. By 'imperialist' is meant, it goes without saying, the imperialism of Paris, not of Berlin or Moscow." The pseudo-pacifists, bloated with hatred for democracy, are the servants of an imposture that is certainly not new.

The unilateralist pacifists condemned the American counterattack in Afghanistan precisely because it *was* a counterattack. The United States, they said, had given in to base desires for revenge. To satisfy their vindictive urges, the Americans had launched an unprovoked air assault that would lead inevitably to the deaths of Afghan civilians. What they should have done was negotiate a political solution. Well, of course! Democracies always refuse to negotiate; only bloodthirsty fanatics are eager to compromise.

The pacifists were forgetting—or rather, deliberately ignoring—the essential point: the purpose of the American reaction was not revenge but defense: the squelching of future terrorism. The world terrorist threat, from which Europe is not exempt, did not end on September 11. In fact, the first chapter of biological terrorism began shortly thereafter. In that tragic time, the democracies could well have been reproached for their failure to read the warning signs, for tardiness in preparing against looming dangers, for having waited until a catastrophe forced them to act. Such procrastination is nothing new; it is an age-old, fatal habit. Was it the United States' fault if Afghanistan was where the jihadists' mastermind was hiding and therefore the place to go looking for him? The intervention in Afghanistan, despite all the precautions taken, could not

---

Il Corriere dell'Umbria, 14 October 2001.

be without danger to civilians; but when the conflict began, it was in New York, not Kabul, that thousands of civilian lives were lost. It seems that for some humanitarians, civilian casualties are indeed acceptable—if they are American casualties.

As for negotiation and the search for a "political solution," I'd like the clever minds who advocate this brilliantly original idea to explain how effective it would be with the likes of Osama bin Laden and Saddam Hussein. Why haven't they proposed to these gentlemen that they participate in an international conference in a neutral country, under the aegis of the United Nations?

In the grim determination to lay blame at the same door, reality is lost from view: the imperatives of chronology, geography and strategy count for nothing. In full anti-American frenzy, some humanitarians lost their heads to the point of accusing the United States of wanting to kill civilians by dropping food packages along with the bombs. A stopgap measure intended to mitigate as far as possible the effects of war—the flow of aid transported by road had been interrupted—the packages were in fact carefully dropped in separate areas. And why wasn't it made clear that the United States had been, from 1980 to 2001, the principal supplier of humanitarian aid to Afghanistan and that 80 percent of the aid distributed by NGOs within the framework of the World Food Program was paid for by Americans? Because to concede as much would have called for a modicum of intellectual integrity.

■ ■ ■

TO AVOID BEING transformed into "aggressors," the Americans would have had to abstain from any retaliation whatsoever against the international terror networks and their chieftains. "To bomb a country back into the Stone Age is absurd; there must be a political solution,"* said, for example, Ihsan Naraghi, a talented Iranian diplomat and intellectual whom, by the way, the ayatollahs of the Islamic Republic had committed to a stretch in prison for political reasons during their revolution. But of course the Americans attacked Afghanistan only because bin Laden and his associates—thanks to the Taliban, with whom it proved useless to negotiate—were sheltering there. It wasn't the Afghan people who were targeted, but the Taliban's military installations, of course. Yet after

---

*Jeune Afrique-l'intelligent, 23 October 2001.

a few days, all we heard was incessant talk of American air attacks and Afghan civilian casualties. The statistics were provided by an obviously tendentious source: the Taliban themselves. (On-the-spot verification by foreign journalists was forbidden.)

The democratic governments for the most part, whatever their differences, never lost sight of the real, life-or-death danger that sooner or later threatened to strike, which in its sheer scale, funding, technical resources, fanaticism and ramifying connections exempted no one. But the media and public opinion, especially in the Muslim countries, came very quickly to regard the intervention in Afghanistan as an isolated phenomenon without any justifying antecedent—a campaign waged not against bin Laden, but against the whole of Islam. And yet fundamentalist Islamo-fascism also threatened several Muslim governments—in Tunisia and Egypt, for example.

On September 11 and 12, faced with the ruins and thousands of dead bodies, "we were all Americans." But forty-eight hours hadn't gone by before discordant notes were heard: Shouldn't we interrogate ourselves on the deeper causes, the roots of the malady that had pushed these young men to their destructive acts? Didn't the U.S.A. share some of the responsibility for its own misfortunes? Couldn't we perhaps be seeing the desperation of poverty in all this?

I have already dealt with and refuted this line of argument. But the nagging question remains: What were the real causes of September 11— something closer to an act of war than an act of terrorism? The fundamental cause is unquestionably located in the resentment felt against the United States, a resentment that grew apace after the collapse of the U.S.S.R. and America's emergence as "sole global superpower." Particularly marked in the Islamic lands—here the existence of Israel, which is blamed on America, plays an important part—the resentment is also more quietly present over the entire planet. In some European capitals, the sense of grievance has been raised to the status of an *idée fixe,* virtually the guiding principle of foreign policy.

Thus the United States is charged with all the evils, real or imagined, that afflict humanity, from the falling price of beef in France to AIDS in Africa and global warming everywhere. The result is a widespread refusal to accept responsibility for one's own actions.

Take the case of Israel. The merits of creating this state in Palestine can be debated, but one thing is certain: it resulted directly from the anti-Semitism of the Europeans. Between the pogroms and the Holocaust, moreover, many more European Jews emigrated to America than to the Middle East. It is true that the United States has supported Israel ever since the latter's birth, but it did not instigate that birth.

As for the American "hyperpower" that causes Europeans so many sleepless nights, they should look to their own history and ask themselves how far they themselves are responsible for that predominance. For it was they who turned the twentieth century into the grimmest in history. It was they who brought about the two apocalypses of the World Wars and invented the two most absurd and criminal political regimes ever inflicted on the human race. If Western Europe in 1945 and Eastern Europe in 1990 were ruined, whose fault was it? American "unilateralism" is the consequence—not the cause—of the other nations' diminished power. Yet it has become habitual to turn the situation around and constantly indict the United States. Is it surprising when such an atmosphere of accumulated hate ends in pushing fanatics to compensate for their failures by engaging in "unilateral" carnage?

Anti-American terrorism, we are constantly being told, can be explained—indeed, justified—on grounds of the "growing poverty" caused by spreading capitalism, whose multinational forces are orchestrated by the United States. This is the refrain of groups like ATTAC* and magazines like *Politis,* of German Greens and Latin American intellectuals and African editorial writers; the radical Left in the United States has made this its rallying cry; it is the conviction of the famous judge Baltasar Garzon, for whom a crime is not a crime unless committed by Pinochet, and of the Nobel Prize winner Dario Fo, who wrote, "What are twenty thousand deaths in New York [*sic*] compared with the millions caused every year by the big speculators?" The awarding of the Nobel Prize for literature to a literary nonentity like Dario Fo had cast doubt on the Stockholm Academy's competence in this subject. At last we can put this doubt to rest: they had actually intended to award him the prize for economics.

Yet the facts are open to everyone: In the last fifty years, in what used to be called the Third World, a threefold increase has occurred: in average income, in population and in life expectancy. This last had more

*A neo-Marxist organization: Action pour une Taxation des Transactions Financières et pour l'Aide aux Citoyens (Alliance for Taxes on Transactions and Aid to Citizens).

than doubled in the developing countries as a whole before AIDS pushed it down again. If Pakistan, which for a long time was ahead of India, today lags behind, it is Zulfikar Ali Bhutto's nationalization policy that should be blamed, not global capitalism. Meanwhile, Bangladesh, despite overpopulation and a lack of natural resources, has been able to achieve self-sufficiency in food production.

As regards the exceptional case of Africa, it bears repeating that the tragic conditions there are attributable to statism rather than liberalism, to socialism rather than capitalism, and to the incessant civil wars that continue to tear the continent apart. The causes of Africa's ruination are more political, ideological and tribal than economic.

Likewise for terrorism. A parallel error made by adherents to the theory of American guilt in all things (the attacks of September 11 not excluded) consists in believing that the roots of terrorism can be severed by a policy of development and modernization, a policy which in any case has been pursued. Basque terrorism owes nothing to poverty—the Basque Country is one of the most prosperous regions in Europe—and the Muslim world includes countries that are among the wealthiest on the planet (especially Saudi Arabia, which finances Osama bin Laden's network and other Islamist organizations in Algeria and Europe). Islamic terrorism in general is the offspring of a religious *idée fixe* and has nothing to do with theories about poverty; and it cannot possibly lead to any improvement in the lot of backward societies. On the contrary, Islamists utterly reject as incompatible with the Qur'an all measures that might contribute to improvement: democracy, secularism, intellectual freedom and critical thought, equality for women, pluralism and openness to other cultures.

Worse: the hyperterrorism launched in New York has indirectly caused a reversal for the world's poorest countries. The economic malaise that it produced among the industrialized nations led to a drop in tourism and curtailment of private investments in the least developed regions of the world, and a cutting back of imports from them. According to the World Bank, related investments fell from $240 billion in 2000 to $160 billion in 2001; and as a result, according to the bank's president, ten million people in the Third World fell below the dollar-a-day income level. Tens of thousands of children were threatened with death by starvation. Hundreds of millions of jobs were wiped out.

After each new wave of terrorism—and they have been frequent, on every continent, over the past thirty years—the same argument has repeatedly been made: one man's terrorist is another man's freedom fighter. During the Occupation, for example, didn't the Gestapo call terrorists those whom the French patriots called resistance fighters? So let's stop classifying as terrorism any violent action that displeases us.

This relativism surfaced again after September 11. Reuters, the British news agency, instructed its journalists to refrain from using the term "terrorist" in connection with September 11 and the suicide pilots. Admirably scrupulous, no doubt, but not particularly helpful. In fact, a terrorist is distinguishable from a freedom fighter on objective grounds.

Violence may be considered legitimate if it is the only way to recover one's freedom—as might be the case under a dictatorship or in a totalitarian state, or when there is a foreign occupying army. But almost none of the terrorist movements active over the past thirty years have arisen in such circumstances. The Red Brigades in Italy, the Red Army Faction in Germany, Direct Action in France, the ETA in the Spanish Basque Country, the Corsican nationalists, the IRA in Northern Ireland, the Peruvian Shining Path—all have engaged in violence in democratic countries where liberty and freedom of speech are institutionally guaranteed, where one can publish newspapers and form political parties, vote, run for office, demonstrate publicly. But the militants do poorly in the polls. Unable to persuade, they murder. Their enemy is not tyranny, it is democracy. For the resistance fighter, the exact opposite is true.

Here, one would think, is a clear and simple standard for identifying the terrorist: far from liberating, he enslaves. And he picks his victims from among ordinary, defenseless citizens. Random assassinations in peacetime, bombs planted in shops and trains, cars loaded with explosives detonated in the streets—this is literally the "terrorizing" of a whole population. In Algeria (not a democratic country), from 1990 to 2000 the Groupe Islamique Armé killed at least 100,000 people. Their preferred victims were not members of the military organization imposing dictatorship, but ordinary villagers who hadn't the slightest political power. The more innocuous they were, the more they were considered desirable targets, since the overall strategy was to create a pervasive climate of fear. The September 11 attacks unquestionably fit this description.

A peculiarity of terrorism is to have vague and indeterminate goals, with no apparent rational link between these goals, however murky, and the acts committed in order to achieve them. If the Baader-Meinhof Gang in Germany and the Red Brigades in Italy imagined they could demolish capitalism by assassinating a few state officials and sowing explosives, they were deluding themselves and revealing how far they had lost contact with reality. And how, during the second *intifada,* was the Palestinian cause helped by massacring teenagers in a disco? Was the objective to consolidate a Palestinian state coexisting with an Israel reduced to its original borders, or was it purely and simply to annihilate Israel and the Israelis, which amounts to the rejection of all past agreements and the promise of war without end? Again, equivocation is the rule.

On the other hand, there is no ambiguity about al-Qaʿida's intentions: it is quite simply to convert the whole of humanity to Islam by force. Just to state such an ambition is to lay bare its irrational and unrealizable absurdity. This is why it is beside the point to rationalize the new terrorism by concrete factors, such as inequalities between nations. The Islamists condemn Westerners, and above all Americans, not because of their wealth, but because they are not Muslims. It is true that they invariably blame the West for their own failures instead of asking themselves why Muslim societies have not successfully entered modernity; but the gravamen of their accusation lies elsewhere. Terrorism is justified in their eyes because it strikes at the infidels who refuse to embrace Islam.

It is not only bin Laden and his emulators and successors who see in the United States an "enemy of Islam that must be destroyed." Even American Muslims, without going to such extremes, believe they must undertake the conversion of their fellow citizens. One of their spokesmen, Siraj Wahaj, who had the honor of being the first Muslim invited to deliver the daily prayer in the House of Representatives, said recently, "If we were united and strong, we'd elect our own emir [leader] and give allegiance to him."*

We deceive ourselves if we think we can negotiate with the al-Qaʿida fanatics and their ilk. For this course to have the remotest chance of success, their motivations would have to be logical. As it is, an abyss separates them from any rational course of action, and terrorism is the parody of policy that serves to fill it.

■ ■ ■

THE DAYS THAT IMMEDIATELY followed the unleashing of the full Islamo-terrorist war against democracy in general and the United States in

---

*Daniel Pipes, "Militant Islam in America," *Commentary,* 12 November 2001.

particular turned out to be an extremely interesting and revealing test-
ing ground, since over a period of two months the phobias and fallacies
of traditional anti-Americanism and of neototalitarianism massively
intensified.

The clumsiest of these fallacies was an attempt to justify Islamist terrorism by claiming that America has long been hostile towards Islam.
But the truth is that the United States' actions historically have been far
less damaging to Muslim interests than the actions of Britain, France or
Russia. These European powers have conquered Muslim countries, occupied and indeed oppressed them over decades and even centuries. Americans, on the other hand, have never colonized a Muslim nation.
Americans evince no hostility towards Islam as such today; on the contrary, their interventions in Somalia, Bosnia and Kosovo, as well as the
pressure exerted on the Macedonian government, were designed to defend
Muslim minorities. And the coalition of twenty-eight countries, led by
the United States, that removed the Iraqi army from Kuwait was formed
at the request of the Saudis, who feared what the Butcher of Baghdad
might do next; so here again the Americans and their allies were defending a small Muslim country against a secular dictator who had used chemical weapons against the Muslim Shi'ites in the south and the Muslim
Kurds in the north. It is strange that America-hating Muslims see nothing disturbing in the fact that Iraq, with a largely Muslim population,
has attacked Muslim countries—first Iran in 1981, then Kuwait in 1990—
in primitively imperialistic and bellicose fashion. Likewise in Algeria,
Muslims have been massacring their coreligionists since 1990.

As I mentioned above, America was not the historical cause of the
emergence of Israel, which arose as a result of endemic European anti-
Semitism. And Muslims may perhaps remember that in 1956 it was the
United States' unilateral intervention that stopped the Anglo-French-
Israeli military operations in Egypt during the Suez Crisis.

Another myth that has been strenuously maintained since September 11 is that of a moderate and tolerant Islam. The myth has three elements, the first of which concerns the history of religions and the exegesis
of sacred texts. It asserts that the Qur'an teaches tolerance and contains
no verses authorizing violence against non-Muslims or apostates. Unfortunately, this soothing canard cannot survive even a cursory examination of Islam's holy book, which on the contrary is riddled with passages
putting believers under an obligation to exterminate infidels. In discus-

sions on this subject after the terrorist attacks, numerous commentators reminded us of this fact, with copious Qur'anic quotations that put it beyond dispute. I will mention only Jacques Rollet's book *Religion et Politique** and an article by Ibn Warraq, "Islam, a Totalitarian Ideology." Ibn Warraq is an Indo-Pakistani and author of *Why I Am Not a Muslim.*** Since the publication of this book, he has been forced to live in hiding (as have Salman Rushdie, author of *The Satanic Verses,* and Taslima Nasreen, a Bangladeshi who in 1993 dared to protest the condition of women under Islam). Were his whereabouts discovered, Ibn Warraq would be assassinated by his tolerant coreligionists. He transcribes an edifying rosary from Qur'anic surahs, for example the following (from Surah 4:76): "Slay the idolaters wherever you find them."

This pious duty was not neglected by the bearded fundamentalists who, on the Sunday of October 28, 2001, at Bahawalpur in Pakistan, burst into a Protestant church during a service. Opening fire with submachine guns, they killed the minister and sixteen of the congregation (four children, seven women and five men) and severely wounded dozens of others, including a two-year-old girl. Surrounded by forty million Muslims, there are about two million Pakistani Christians, Catholic and Protestant, who obviously cannot even remotely be guilty of the evil actions imputed to the West by the Islamist fanatics; so clearly it was for their status as infidels that these innocent people were murdered. Bin Laden had commanded: "Slay the Christians!" He was heard. (Apropos of "innocent victims," I haven't heard that the European Left shed many tears over these Christian Pakistanis.)

The dominant idea in the Muslims' worldview is that all of humanity must obey the rules of *their* religion, whereas they owe no respect to the religions of others. Indeed, showing such respect would make them apostates meriting instant execution. Muslim "tolerance" is a one-way street: they demand it for themselves but rarely extend it to others.

Anxious to show tolerance, the Pope permitted—even encouraged—the erection of a mosque in Rome, the city where Saint Peter is buried. But no Christian church could be built in Mecca, or anywhere in Saudi Arabia, for that would profane the land of Muhammad. In October 2001, Islamic opinion—echoed by voices in the West—continually asked the

---

*Grasset, 2001. See also this author's comments in *Le Point,* 21 September 2001.
**Prometheus Books, 1995.

American administration to suspend military operations during the month of Ramadan, which was to begin in mid-November. War or no war, decency requires that holy days be accorded proper consideration—so said these well-intentioned people. A fine precept, except that Muslims consider themselves exempt from it. In 1973, Egypt didn't hesitate to attack Israel on the day of Yom Kippur, the most important Jewish religious holiday, thus initiating what will be known forever as the Yom Kippur War.

The second element in the myth of a tolerant Islam is the claim that the bulk of the Muslim populations, especially those resident in or citizens of European countries or America, disapprove of terrorism. The imams of the principal mosques in the West have made a specialty of dispensing these suave assurances. After each wave of murderous attacks, for example in France in 1986 and 1995, and after the *fatwas* (in 1989 and 1993) ordering Salman Rushdie and Taslima Nasreen to be killed for their "blasphemies," these spokesmen tripped over themselves as they rushed to guarantee the essential moderateness of the communities under their spiritual leadership. Politicians and the media hastened to fall into line, so fearful are we of appearing racist. Thus Ibn Warraq aptly remarks: "The Westerners' cowardice frightens me as much as the Islamists do."

On September 12, 2001, the newspaper *Le Parisien-Aujourd'hui* published an account of the jubilant atmosphere that reigned the previous evening in the 18th *arrondissement,* where there is a large Muslim community. "Bin Laden will nail all of you! He started with America, then it'll be France." Such was the sort of moderate remark hurled at passersby who didn't look like North Africans. Or again: "I'm going to celebrate big time tonight! Those guys were real heroes. That'll teach those Americans—and all you French are next!"

This reportage by the *Parisien* had no equivalent in any other publication and was passed over in silence by almost all the media. At any rate, as an assiduous listener every morning to news and press summaries on the radio, I heard no mention of it on the morning of the 12th.

While the statistics are unreliable, it's thought that between four and five million Muslims are living in France. This is the largest such community in Europe, followed a long way behind by those in Germany and Britain. If the "immense majority" of these Muslims are moderates, as the imams and muftis and their political and media parrots claim, it seems to me that this moderation should be rather more apparent. For example, after the bombings of 1986 and 1995 in Paris, which killed several dozen people and wounded many more, it should have been easy to find a few thousand "moderates" out of 4.5 million Muslims, a good proportion of whom have French nationality—enough at least for a demonstration march from the République to the Bastille or along the Canebière. There was never even a hint of one.

In Spain, there were several rallies of up to a hundred thousand people in 2001 to condemn the assassins of the Basque ETA terrorist organization. These took place throughout the country and even in the Basque Country, where protestors had reason to fear reprisals, although the terrorists' partisans were actually very much in the minority (which was made overwhelmingly evident by the regional elections of November 2000).

In contrast, if moderate Muslims in France dare to protest publicly so little, couldn't it be because they know that they, and not the extremists, are minorities within their communities? This explains why they are so moderate with their moderation. It's the same story in Britain, where in 1989 Muslims, for the most part Pakistani immigrants, erupted with anger against Salman Rushdie and shouted for his death, with nary a protest against such barbarity. And after September 11, a qualified spokesman for British Muslims, a certain al-Misri, called the attacks on the World Trade Center acts of "legitimate defense." Another spiritual authority, Omar Bakri Mohammed, launched a *fatwa* commanding the assassination of the president of Pakistan because the latter had sided with President Bush against bin Laden.* However attentively you might have listened, you would never have heard the slightest whisper from moderate British Muslims protesting against the calls for murder. There were no such protests, just as there is no such thing as a moderate Muslim majority in France. The notion that the "immense majority" of Muslims settled in Europe were peacefully inclined was, during the two months after September 11, starkly revealed for what it was: a mirage.

President Bush did right when, the day after the attacks, he solemnly proclaimed that he was confident of American Muslims' patriotism; and he did right to visit mosques in order to underline this confidence. It was essential to calm emotions that, given the staggering proportions of the crime, might have been directed against Arab-Americans. The president

---

Le Point, 2 November 2001.

acted in the best democratic moral tradition. And several European heads of state and prime ministers wisely did the same. This democratic observance does honor to Americans and Europeans, but should not blind them to the hatred that the majority of Muslims living among us feel for the West.

After September 11, democratic leaders took great care to stress that the West's war against terrorism was not a war against Islam. But for their part, the Islamists made no bones about proclaiming that they were fighting against the West. Their objective is, of course, the fruit of a delusion, but it remains well and truly the destruction of Western civilization in all its impiety and impurity. For this reason, attempts to blame hyperterrorism on American hyperpower and capitalist globalization—to ascribe rational economic and political causes to it—must be completely groundless. The fundamentalists blame our civilization not for what it does, but for what it is; not for having failed, but for having succeeded. So the endless talk about the need to find a "political solution" to the problem of Islamist terrorism is founded on the illusion that rational policy could have any bearing on a mental universe so divorced from reality.

A manual handed out to apprentice jihadists in bin Laden's training camps—an English translation circulates in Britain—unequivocally states the principles and aims of the holy war. The philosophical references it contains show that the authors cannot be dismissed as untutored village idiots; they have evidently studied in Western universities. They spell out their position in full knowledge of the facts:

> The confrontation with the apostate regimes we are calling for has nothing to do with Socratic debates, Platonic ideals and Aristotelian diplomacy. It holds, rather, to the ideals of assassination, bombs and destruction, to the diplomacy of the rifle and submachine gun. The principal mission of our military organization is to overthrow the Godless regimes and replace them all with an Islamic regime.

This is but one specimen from an outpouring of similar exhortations. These are calls to annihilate our civilization and our ways of thinking. These people are not concerned about regulating global trade or increasing aid to the developing countries; their one idea is to extirpate Evil from the earth and replace it with Good, i.e. Islam.

At home, moreover, the enemies of democracy know the game. Young people of the extreme Right, followers of Jean-Marie Le Pen, celebrated with champagne in offices of the National Front as they watched televised images of the Twin Towers collapsing in flames. At the other end of the political spectrum: delegates from the Confédération Générale du Travail, the Communist trade union, at celebrations sponsored by *L'Humanité* on September 16, booed the national secretary of the Communist Party, Robert Hue, when he called for three minutes of silence in memory of the murdered Americans. This is the same hostility towards democratic civilization that prompted North African spectators of French nationality to boo the traditional *Marseillaise* played before the soccer match between France and Algeria on October 6.

In addition to these outbursts, from leftist political and intellectual milieus came some more nuanced reactions that nevertheless tended to insinuate that the jihadist attacks were not morally unjustified. It's worth noting that all these anti-American viewpoints began to circulate freely before October 7, 2001, meaning before the campaign to dislodge the Taliban had begun. After that date, the bombing became the most frequently invoked reason to take sides against the Americans; but this was just one more element in an indictment that from the beginning laid the blame on America as the model par excellence of capitalist democracy and "materialistic" civilization. Everyone knows that the purest unselfishness reigns in Africa and Asia, especially in the Muslim nations, and that the universal corruption that is ravaging them is the expression of a high spirituality.

A good many sensible people, while not falling into such pathological rancor, made statements that hinted at the same set of ideas. The French prime minister, Lionel Jospin, seemed to be discreetly pointing in this direction when he asked, "What lesson are the Americans going to draw from what has happened?" The lesson, Jospin indicated, should be for the United States to moderate her unilateralism.

Now, perhaps the United States *is* guilty of "unilateralism"; but the question to ask is whether the terrorist destruction of the tallest American skyscrapers was an appropriate response. While declaring Franco-American solidarity in the war against terrorism, Jospin did not therefore dismiss entirely the idea that the punishment inflicted on America was not undeserved. Going further, an ATTAC spokesman quoted the adage: "He who sows the wind shall reap the whirlwind." This opinion was widespread, to judge from many statements reported by the media; and it was evidently shared by the so-called Muslim "moderates" of France,

Britain and elsewhere, even if, according to opinion polls, they did condemn the *principle* of terrorism. But did they condemn the practice? Apparently not.

In any case, if globalization is condemned by the elites of the Left, it is adopted without false shame by the Islamists as long as it's the Islamic kind. "ISLAM WILL DOMINATE THE WORLD"—such was the slogan on signs held aloft by Islamist demonstrators of British nationality as they marched in October 2001 to Luton (north of London). Right-thinking Westerners are mistaking their own wishes for realities—or their listeners for dupes—when they claim to be convinced of the fundamental tolerance of the Islamic world. One might have thought that a good many Muslims, while rightly or wrongly holding Westerners responsible for the difficulties and backwardness of Islamic countries, would nevertheless condemn terrorism as a criminal absurdity that can do nothing to solve their problems. If such Muslims exist, we hardly heard from them. Muslim political leaders in Pakistan and Saudi Arabia who, for reasons of diplomacy and strategy, did condemn the attacks have paid for their daring by sacrificing their popularity.

Throughout the world, during the two months following September 11, a large section of public opinion, "experts" and media pundits evolved towards the following position, implied if not explicitly stated: the real aggression was not the hyperterrorists' attacks but the United States' response in Afghanistan. Naturally, this version of events had been heard all along from the majority of Muslims. But the interesting thing is that eventually it spread fairly widely in the West. The more moderate critics vaguely admitted that America had been attacked; but they focused principally on the danger of civilian deaths in Afghanistan, of creating a "humanitarian catastrophe." The risk was only too tragically real; and that every precaution had to be taken to spare the populace and aid refugees was perfectly obvious. But "unilateralism" had to be severe indeed for the blame for this situation to be laid solely at America's door. The unhappy Afghan population had been suffering for twenty years from the crimes committed, first by the Red Army and then by the Taliban fanatics. Since 1980, starving Afghans had streamed out of the country seeking refuge. But for many people, the horrors only began in 2001 with the United States' military operations.

The conclusion to be drawn from all this is clear. According to the anointed Western *bien pensants,* the United States is the only nation without the right to defend itself against enemy aggression. One of the most dishonest objections raised against the right to legitimate self-defense consists in saying that the Americans made use of bin Laden during the Afghans' war of resistance against the U.S.S.R.—even that he was initiated into combat (shocking!) by the CIA. (The United States is, as everyone knows, the only country in the world to have secret agencies.) But what was extraordinary or reprehensible about Ronald Reagan's accepting the services of all those willing to oppose the Soviet Union, not excepting Muslims? Was it necessary to wait until all the Afghans and Saudis had read Montesquieu and converted to Christianity before they could be recruited? Imagine for a moment what it would have meant for India, Pakistan and the Gulf countries—for all of us, in fact—if the Soviets had been able to achieve a permanent takeover of Afghanistan. There would have been no Gorbachev, no glasnost, no perestroika. Coming from the Europeans, who at the time were quivering in cowardice and debating only if they should or shouldn't participate in the Moscow Olympic Games (thanks to Georges Marchais, France hastened to do so), this critique about the possible ties between the CIA and bin Laden has something, one might say, backward about it.

One Western reaction to the hyperterrorist war was its co-option by the antiglobalizers. Granted, at first even these people were stunned by the magnitude of the 9/11 crimes and reduced to silence by the wave of solidarity with the Americans. For a few days, anti-Americanism had a bad press. But for a few days only. Very soon the notion emerged that "bin Laden is joining the antiglobalists' struggle."* For Cardinal Karl Lehmann, president of the German Bishops' Conference, the lesson to be drawn from terrorism was that "the West must not seek to dominate the rest of the world."** And for Ulrich Beck, professor of sociology at the University of Munich, the attacks marked "the end of neoliberalism." Though none of the texts in which the Islamists set out the motives for their actions make any mention of a war on liberalism, it is nevertheless the misdeeds of the latter that explain the attacks, according to many representatives of the European Left.

---

*This is how the weekly *Jeune Afrique-l'intelligent* phrased it in their 23 October 2001 issue.
**Le Figaro,* 3 November 2001.

With persistent hypocrisy, the antiglobalists more than ever blamed Third World poverty on free trade, whereas the underdeveloped countries themselves keep complaining about barriers that prevent or limit the export of their agricultural products and textiles to the industrialized nations. The European Union in particular, whose farmers derive half of their income from subsidies, takes the lead in this protectionism, which moreover encourages an overproduction that severely hurts the taxpayer. Nothing could more clearly illustrate the antiglobalists' utter incoherence: while grandstanding as champions of the world's poorest nations, they spurn the free trade that these nations are clamoring for. The Cairns Group of countries was formed in 1986 in Cairns, Australia, with the express purpose of promoting market-oriented policies and the liberalization of trade rules. Among the seventeen member nations are Argentina, Brazil, Chile, Colombia, Indonesia, the Philippines and Thailand, whose economies rely heavily on agricultural exports. Accordingly, in November 2001, at the summit meeting of the World Trade Organization in Doha, the capital of Qatar, the Cairns Group fought to include in the day's agenda at least a *gradual* reduction in the subsidies and protectionist measures that enrich the developed nations. The E.U., yet again, discussed the subject only reluctantly, while in classic fashion throwing responsibility for protectionism back on the United States. No surprise here.

Commenting on the summit's stakes, the French economic minister, Laurent Fabius, unburdened himself of this strange analysis: "We must take action against the inequalities that feed terrorism; we must exercise control over globalization." Which shows how an intelligent man who is far from being an extremist can subscribe to the antiglobalist doctrine according to which Islamist hyperterrorism is caused by free trade, which therefore, despite the pleas of the emerging countries, must be curtailed. And since, as ATTAC maintains, the "war [in Afghanistan] is at the frontline of the campaign to establish world liberalization," that is reason enough to oppose it.*

In any case, the antiglobalists must have been delighted with the results of terrorism, since the September 11 attacks caused a worldwide

---

*This nugget is extracted from a bulletin of the ATTAC group quoted in an article by John Vinocour, "War Transforms the Anti-Globalization Crowd," *International Herald Tribune*, 2 November 2001.

recession; and inevitably, alas, we saw a dramatic drop in exports from the developing nations, the disappearance of tens of millions of jobs, and attendant increases in poverty and hunger.* This small inconvenience associated with liberal globalization's retrenchment seems to have escaped the antiglobalizers' notice.

Likewise, although the renewed deterioration of Israeli-Palestinian relations after 2000 has incontestably added fuel to the anti-Israel hatred felt by a large part of the Arab world, the question of Israel does not seem to be in the forefront of al-Qaʿida's ideology. The militants' "theoretical" texts attest much more to their hatred for Jews in general than for Israel in particular. Furthermore, given the complexity and scale of the operation, it seems evident that September 11 was conceived and initiated well before the beginning of the second *intifada* and Ariel Sharon's coming to power. It has been rightly noted that the first terrorist attack against the World Trade Center—the 1993 car bomb atrocity, which today we know was the work of bin Laden's network—occurred just as the peace process envisioning the creation of a Palestinian state had begun in Oslo. Islamists of the bin Laden stripe scorn all compromise and aim at much more than just Israel: it is the whole of modern civilization that is their target.

In their eyes, this civilization is intrinsically and, so to speak, metaphysically incompatible with Islam. The Americans "are everywhere attacking Muslims": this paranoid fantasy of bin Laden's, repeated by his followers, was an *a posteriori* attempt to concoct empirical pretexts for their transcendentally derived project of extermination. As bin Laden clarified: "The real targets of the attacks were the icons of American military and economic power."* To a journalist who objected that hundreds of Muslims died when the Twin Towers collapsed, he replied: "The Islamic *sharia* says that Muslims ought not live in the land of the infidels for an extended time." Thus the Muslim victims only got what they deserved. Clearly, a critique of neoliberalism hardly counts as a priority of the neo-Islamists.

---

*A communiqué from the World Bank on 1 October 2001 stated: "Poverty has been on the increase from the day after the terrorist attacks on the U.S.A. Millions more human beings will be condemned to poverty in 2002."

**From an interview given by bin Laden to two Pakistani dailies on 9 November 2001; reprinted in *Le Monde,* 11–12 November 2001.

The extent and significance of the changes brought about by the "new war" declared on the democracies—and on several other states that are not democratic but have made the mistake of being allied to the democracies—cannot be underestimated. This unprecedented and unforeseen aggression, in its manner as well as in its extent, has no doubt lastingly changed the idea that the United States has of herself and her relations with the world; it has brought about a transformation, as rapid as it is profound, of international relations and strategic ideas. These changes must be studied and assessed over the long term. But they have little to do with the reactionary imaginings of the antiglobalists, anticapitalists and antiliberals.

4. The Worst Society That Ever Was

THE VERDICT DELIVERED AGAINST the United States, mainly in Europe and especially by France (which wields the loudest bullhorn on this subject) does not bear only on the hyperpower's unilateralism—an indictment curiously linked, when the need arises, with that of isolationism. It also sweepingly condemns American society as such, branding it as practically the worst association of human beings that history has ever seen.

What picture of American society is likely to be imprinted on the consciousness of average Europeans? If they happen to be French, they can hardly have any choice in the unpleasant particulars, given what they read or hear every day from intellectuals and politicians. That picture is as follows:

In the first place, American society is entirely ruled by money. No other value, whether familial, moral, religious, civic, cultural, professional or ethical, has any currency in itself. All these values are brought back to money. Everything is a commodity, regarded and used exclusively as a commodity. A person is judged solely by the worth of his bank account. Every president has been in the pockets of the oil companies, the military-industrial complex, the agricultural lobby or the financial manipulators of Wall Street. America is the "jungle" par excellence of out-of-control liberalism and "savage" capitalism, where the rich are always becoming richer and always fewer while the poor are always becoming poorer and always more numerous. Poverty is the dominant social reality in America. Hordes of famished indigents are everywhere, while luxurious chauffeured limousines with darkened windows glide through the urban wilderness.

77

Poverty and inequality like this should rightfully cause Europeans to cringe in horror, especially since (we have it on good authority) there is no social security in America, no unemployment benefits, no retirement, no assistance for the destitute—not the slightest bit of social solidarity. Europeans firmly believe this caricature because it is repeated every day by the elites. Only the rich can afford medical care, because for doctors, as for everyone else in America, profit is the sole motive. University courses—a privilege, not a right—are reserved only for those who can pay, which partly explains the low level of education in the U.S.A., along with the notoriously mediocre elementary and secondary schooling in that benighted land.

Another distinctive feature of the United States: the pandemic violence. Everywhere you go, violence reigns, with uniquely high levels of delinquency and criminality and a feverish state of near-open revolt in the ghettos. This last is the inevitable result of the deep-rooted racism of American society, which sets ethnic "communities" one against the other, and ethnic minorities as a whole against the oppressive white majority. And the unpardonable cowardice—coupled with venality, obviously—that has prevented political elites from banning the sale of firearms results in periodic, appalling bloodbaths when teenagers mercilessly gun down their teachers and fellow students in the classroom.

Yet another universally held conviction is that these social ills are all the more unlikely to be cured insofar as Americans make it a point of honor to elect only mental defectives as presidents. From the Missouri tie salesman Truman to the Texas cretin George W. Bush, not to mention the peanut farmer Carter and the B-movie actor Reagan, the White House offers us a gallery of nincompoops. Only John F. Kennedy, in the eyes of the French, rose a little above this undistinguished bunch, probably because he had the merit of having married someone of French extraction; naturally, this union could not fail to raise President Kennedy's intelligence to at least average level—doubtless too high for his fellow citizens, who never forgave him for this and ended up assassinating him.

In any case, everyone knows that the U.S.A. is a democracy only in appearance: in the 1950s the real face of the American political system was revealed during the McCarthy episode. Of course, it's entirely irrelevant that McCarthy came to be strongly disapproved even by American conservatives, and that the Senate, in December 1954, censured him by 67 votes against 22, effectively destroying the strident senator's political career; it still remains axiomatic that McCarthy reveals the inner essence of the regime created by the Constitution of the United States. It is forgotten that the House Committee on Un-American Activities was originally created in 1937 to combat the Ku Klux Klan, which was considered an anti-American organization because it rejected the constitutional contract that lies at the heart of the American system.

Another example showing the supposed hollowness of American democracy: the November 2000 political cliffhanger between George W. Bush and Al Gore was routinely derided, in the phrase-of-choice trotted out on the airwaves, as a "Hollywood soap opera"—the presupposition being, by the way, that Hollywood has never produced anything but tripe.

■ ■ ■

SUCH AN ACCOUNT, filled with distortions as it is, reflects more on the psychological problems of those who proffer it than on the failures of the society put in the dock. Despite the ever-growing availability of information and the ever-decreasing cost of travel, the reigning absurdities in conventional European judgments on the United States have barely changed since the days when I catalogued them in 1970 in *Without Marx or Jesus.*

It cannot be repeated often enough that every society has its share of real faults and ignominies, which observers are at liberty to describe and condemn. But the standard indictments of the United States wheel out the same small set of platitudes that reveal an ignorance of the subject so crude one can only hope it's intentional. Thus, a certain Jean-Marc Adolphe, replying to an article by Jacques Julliard in *Libération*, reproached him for considering America a democracy; it clearly isn't one, he said, since in America "only the most fortunate have the right to medical care and grow old with dignity."* Now, if Americans for the most part are covered by an insurance system whose premiums, shared by employers and employees, are not more burdensome than the equivalent deductions by the French state, it is also true that *public* expenditures on health care in the U.S. represent a percentage of gross domestic product that is approximately equal to France's.

**Libération*, 14–15 November 2001.

Health care in the United States certainly has deficiencies; but if French health care does not, why did the Jospin government feel obligated to create the CMU (Couverture Maladie Universelle), when we learned that six million people—one-tenth of the population—had until then no access to health-care services? And when Adolphe makes his comment about aging "with dignity," he probably means that public-supported retirement (instituted by Franklin D. Roosevelt in the 1930s) is unheard-of in America.

The question of medical care at least has the merit of bearing on specific facts. Preferring vaguer themes, Adolphe goes on to assert that America cannot be a democracy because it is a nation "where everything can be bought and sold." Moreover, he says, the power of U.S. judges is excessive—as is often claimed—or on the other hand, that America is a lawless jungle. So which is it? There *is* law in the U.S., Adolphe concedes, but it is a "law of the *producteur* rather than of the *auteur*." What on earth can this mean? That there are no publishing contracts in the United States? That literary and artistic copyright is not protected? That the history of American literature and cinema is an arid desert, devoid of original talent or great creators, these having been constantly shackled by those pesky "producers"?

European literary figures are not alone in despising American authors, to whom, nevertheless, they owe so many renewing themes and revolutionary narrative techniques. The daily newspaper *Asahi Shimbun,* interviewing Japanese writers and philosophers after September 11, recorded not only political attitudes leaning more towards the jihadists than their victims, but literary judgments imbued with condescension and assurance of superiority.* The philosopher Yujiro Nakamura issues this pronouncement:

> American culture has always glorified physical and mental health and disdained what hides amid the shadows of human nature: the weaknesses and shortcomings. . . . Human beings are weak, but American culture ignores their dark dimension because it contributes nothing to productivity and efficiency. Such a civilization is the vehicle for a unidimensional vision of the world that strives to avoid awareness of the abysses that men carry within themselves.

---

*"Des intellectuals japonais s'interrogent sur la guerre en Afghanistan," *Le Monde,* 11 December 2001.

Evidently, Nakamura has never read Melville, Poe, Hawthorne, Henry James, Faulkner, Tennessee Williams or the Scott Fitzgerald of *The Crack Up,* to mention only a few explorers of the depths.

Most of the intellectuals consulted did not fail to make ritual denunciations of American "arrogance," adding that the very wealth of America disqualifies her from speaking in the name of human rights. Everyone knows that Japan has always been deeply respectful towards the latter, as Koreans, Chinese and Filipinos can amply confirm. In fact, we find no mention in Japanese textbooks of any atrocities that might have been committed by the imperial armies before and during World War II. (Patriotic discretion demands that they be passed over in silence.) Thus do Japanese scholars, in their distinct fashion, serve the cause of truth in the discipline of historiography, with the dignified modesty that has always graced Japan.

What's more, American writers are far more critical of their own society than the anti-American parrots proclaim. The years from 1865 to 1914, the period from the end of the Civil War to the beginning of World War I, known as the Gilded Age—with its frenetic industrialization, money-making and Robber Barons—gave rise to several novelists who depicted their society as corrupt, vulgar, uncultivated, materialistic and hypocritically puritanical. Among them were Frank Norris, Theodore Dreiser, Upton Sinclair and Sinclair Lewis, whose books were just as harshly accusatory of American society as were Zola's of French society. These authors owed many of their themes to a new form of journalism that was scrupulous in gathering facts and free from editorial censorship; often muckraking, yet often idealistic, this investigative journalism was another manifestation of the American self-critical spirit.

Of course, the tradition of social criticism in literature by no means dried up in 1914. Steinbeck and Dos Passos, among other writers of the "lost generation," sustained it between the wars, the latter with his powerful *U.S.A.* trilogy. After 1945, the tradition mutated but remained no less vital, with the work of such novelists as John Updike and Tom Wolfe reflecting rapidly changing problems and evolving attitudes. Likewise in American film and television, which are far more willing to confront sensitive social or political issues (Watergate is the classic example) than are European productions. The idea that American literature and cinema are entirely dedicated to narcissistic fantasies about the American Dream and American excellence is the product of hallucination.

■ ■ ■

THE AVERAGE EUROPEAN is likely to sneer that America, a society still in a primitive state, ruled by violence and criminality, couldn't possibly have a mature culture.

The first misunderstanding about violence in the United States stems from the fact that the English word "crime" can refer to all sorts of infractions and misdemeanors, including the most minor, whereas the French word *"crime"* denotes, above all, homicide. When a European, with a blend of horror and secret satisfaction, reads U.S. crime statistics, what he usually doesn't know is that "criminality" covers everything from theft and passing bad checks, or selling marijuana in the streets or siphoning gasoline from a neighbor's car, to bank robbery and first-degree murder.

This point established, it remains true nevertheless that American society has always been a violent one—a reality that Americans are fully aware of and strive to mitigate. Americans do not deny the existence of crime, as Europeans too often are likely to do regarding their own social problems. The French especially have for a long time closed their eyes to their own rapidly rising crime levels. The result is that during the final fifteen years of the twentieth century, crime steadily diminished in the United States, whereas in Europe it took off.* The most famous American achievement in this regard is the "New York Miracle," when Rudolph Giuliani, elected mayor in 1993, succeeded over a period of five years in cutting by half the previously very high levels of crime and delinquency in that city.

Giuliani, who at first was mocked in certain French newspapers that subtly dubbed him "Giussolini," a slur on his Italian origins, quickly left dumbfounded the leaders of other big American cities that had been rendered unlivable by crime and could do nothing with their placebo remedies. Unlike Mussolini, Mayor Giuliani never promoted a policy of repressive brutality, although there were one or two serious police blunders, the kind that befalls police in every country through accident or ineptitude, especially in the least effective police forces. His strategy, based on the principle he called "zero tolerance," consisted in punishing *every* infraction, even the most minimal—purse-snatching, bicycle theft,

---

*These figures can be found in Alain Bauer and Emile Pérez, *L'Amérique, la violence, le crime, les réalités et les mythes* (PUF, 2000).

subway gate-jumping, even graffiti. If criminality was not nipped in the bud, he said, it would only grow and produce zones of lawlessness—the kind that disfigures France today. Another Giuliani principle is the "broken window effect." The expression originated in an article by sociologists James Q. Wilson and George L. Kelling. According to their analysis, if a window pane that has been broken by vandals is not immediately replaced, and if the vandals are not immediately arrested and punished, the whole block, and then the neighborhood, may eventually be trashed and taken over by gangs that the police will not be able to control. Roles will be reversed: the gangs will hunt down the police—a scenario that became, from around 1980 onwards, part of the French civic landscape.

After having refused for two decades to recognize even the existence of a domestic security problem, then having finally consented to see it, the French Left at first threw itself into what it called a purely "preventive" policy, which in fact prevented nothing. So they ended up doing a sharp U-turn in 2001. To get an idea of the magnitude of the policy change, it suffices to glance at the headlines of the December 4, 2001, issue of *Le Monde:* "THE LEFT NO LONGER FAVORS SOCIAL EXPLANATIONS OF DELINQUENCY." And the headline that topped the page, "ZERO TOLERANCE: THE NEW WATCHWORD ON CRIME CONTROL," was followed by the extended subtitle: "Tried out in New York under Rudolph Giuliani's leadership, a policy of systematic suppression of petty crime is now held up as an example by numerous elected officials. A new way of thinking about the handling of juvenile violence." A boxed summary in midpage spotlighted the Broken Window doctrine.

Even among socialists, who thus confessed their—I quote—"naïve optimism," leniency towards antisocial behaviors was no longer acceptable. The socialist prime minister, Lionel Jospin, declared, "Every act that is not respectful of the law must be appropriately punished." To have acknowledged this premise after twenty years of error was particularly impressive. Yet the minister of justice, Marylise Lebranchu, haughtily proclaimed, "The government has no desire to copy the American model." One has one's pride and one's scruples, after all.

Nobody will fail to admire the exquisite contradiction in this line of reasoning. It is not contested anymore, even in France, that the United States succeeded in reducing its crime levels between 1990 and 2000, whereas during the same period, crime levels in France and in Europe overall kept climbing. Overwhelmed by their failure to combat this curse, and unable to hide from the obvious forever, the French authorities in 2001 were forced to acknowledge that their analysis of crime's causes had long been flawed, and that their remedies, based upon supposed prevention, didn't work. The French Left, sheepishly followed by the Right, was forced to admit that Giuliani's method was not *all* bad; it had been imitated, moreover, with the same convincing results in many other American cities. But although won over to this method under the pressure of facts, the French—or at least the French political class—nonetheless insisted on proclaiming that they would *not* be converted to the "American model." What model? This was just a pompous term for measures that were really based on elementary common sense, dictated by experience.

As a thought experiment, and to mention another area in which France can lay claim to a disastrous record, imagine that she reduced the number of auto accident victims through effective enforcement of speed limits by a police force present on the highways rather than just on television. Would something like this be a servile aping of the "American model" and therefore a deplorable policy? Or would it be a government simply doing its duty?

So one sees how anti-Americanism serves as an excuse for government incompetence, ideological backwardness and criminal disorder. We choose well in rejecting the American model, even if our choice leads to shipwreck.

This pout of disdain for American solutions, in law enforcement and many other social and economic areas, on the part of numerous countries that do much less well than the U.S.A. verges on ineptitude and even absurdity. For, particularly in matters relating to law and order, it is not so much a question of whether France *should* follow the American model, but of whether she is capable of doing so. On January 4, 2002, a journalist on RTL radio, interviewing the mayor of Amiens, which is among the cities hardest hit by street crime, charitably warned the mayor about the risk of transforming himself into an "American-style sheriff." Prime Minister Lionel Jospin had already, six months earlier, contemptuously made this comparison of a mayor to a sheriff when refusing to grant French mayors the police powers they had held before 1939, which were taken away by the Vichy regime. It was surprising to hear a Socialist prime minister defend a police hypercentralism that had been introduced into France by a dictatorship, but identifying the American office of mayor with the sheriff's revealed a remarkable but not exceptional ignorance of American institutions. A sheriff (a word borrowed from English common law) in the United States is an elected county officer charged with maintaining order and enforcing respect for judicial decisions. His role is far more restricted than that of the mayor, whose duties and powers within the municipality are much greater and extend to more numerous and varied domains. This is like confusing the mayor of a large French town with a captain of the Gendarmerie.

It can be maintained that Giuliani's tactics had some dark areas and were not a complete success in New York or places where they were imitated. The trouble is that this critique is hardly legitimate coming from France, insofar as our policies during the same decade were a complete failure. While crime and delinquency in America receded, in France they doubled between 1985 and 1998. Since then they have been galloping ahead even faster. An insight: one inhabitant of Vitry-sur-Seine, deploring the steep rise in car-burnings in his neighborhood, cried, "It's worse here than in America!"

But America can no longer be used as a benchmark—France has left it so far behind. In 2000, in the *département* of Val-de-Marne alone, armed assaults increased by 60 percent. And the majority of crimes and misdemeanors are not reported; these are what the Ministry of the Interior calls the "shadow statistics." What is most disturbing is that this increase, including everything from sexual "incivilities" (as they are euphemistically termed) to murder, marks the entrance onto the scene of younger and younger perpetrators, and from distinctly untraditional milieus. An educator in Vitry-sur-Seine said to *Le Point,* "They leave school without a diploma and with an educational level close to zero. From the age of ten, they settle into the underground economy. They don't know how to do anything else. Armed robbery is the logical end result."

This damning statement, by a witness who is in a position to know, underscores another monumental failure of the French state: national education. Reversing the course of what has been the successful theory and practice of educators for three thousand years or more,* our anointed totalitarians saw fit to banish, from 1970 onwards, two "abuses" they

---

*See Henri-Irénée Marrou's classic *Histoire de l'éducation dans L'Antiquité* (Seuil, 1948).

considered intolerable: teaching factual knowledge and enforcing class-room discipline.

Violence in schools—or, to put it plainly, crime—is one of the most ominous consequences of our pedagogic irresponsibility. For a time this mayhem affected only *lycées* and *collèges* (state secondary schools). There is a logic to this, since one supposes that students would have to be at least twelve or thirteen years old before being able to use knives and handguns. There were repeated protests by schoolteachers who were tired of being attacked in class without provocation or seeing teenagers being beaten up and sometimes killed. But it was not until 2001 that such barbarity began to spread into elementary schools among children less than eight years old, who could be extremely violent towards each other and their teachers. Around the end of November 2001, in the 20th *arrondissement* of Paris and in L'Hay-les-Roses (Val-de-Marne), two children ages seven and eight assaulted their female instructors. Naturally, the subject is taboo, as the Ministry of Education is bent on "relativizing" the problem away; parents who wish to lodge complaints are dissuaded by the administration in the name of a healthy code of tolerance, solidarity and social awareness.

Unhappily, hypocrisy is powerless to suppress the rampant violence, and schoolteachers are resorting more and more to the only means they have of shaking the authorities' inertia: strikes. The ever-growing difficulty in maintaining orderly classes has made the strikes more or less permanent. One example drawn at random from the press: The faculty of the Victor Hugo secondary school in Noisy-le-Grand (Seine-Saint-Denis), outraged by the "daily harassment" they received from pupils, estimated that "two-thirds of the classes are unmanageable." They wrote to the prime minister requesting an audience with the president of the Republic in order to demand the "abandonment of the educational policies implemented in France during the last twenty years."*

This is a new and major theme, the more significant inasmuch as one of the pretexts for the French derision of the United States is the supposedly lamentable state of the American educational system. But it was in France, again in Noisy-le-Grand, that a mother, bemoaning a strike's implications for her child's education, was told by a teacher, "Whether classes are held or not, the students don't learn much anyway." And if a student evinces a desire to learn, some thug in the class is likely

---

Le Monde, 22 December 2001.

to bring him back to reason with a beating. In one suburban secondary school, a pupil seated in the first row, wanting to follow the instruction, turned towards his fellow students and asked them to quiet down. He was assaulted and had a chair broken over his head, sustaining a wound that required stitches and ten days out of school.* A twenty-nine-year-old teacher of history and geography bitterly observed: "The law says that a student can call us whores and fascists, and he can't be punished." All these educators put in relief the link between the anti-educational and anti-law-and-order ideologies that, in twenty years, have combined to plunge France into a condition close to anarchy.

Europeans are right to criticize the freedom to sell firearms that prevails in the United States. But their vituperations would be more convincing if it were not just as easy to procure weapons in Europe, on a flourishing black market; although firearms cannot be freely bought and sold, the result is the same, if not worse. The arms trafficking is "phenomenal" in Seine-Saint-Denis, said a leader of the Force police union on the Europe 1 radio station in November 2001. "In the *département* of Seine-Saint-Denis," he said, "two weeks ago we found military weapons in La Courneuve, and in Épinay." The officially condoned selling of arms to individuals in America at least makes provision for the registration of the purchaser's name, who must also pay for a license and be fingerprinted. It is in Europe that an arms traffic jungle, the kind in which anyone can obtain the most lethal weapons without anyone else knowing about it, is growing unchecked.

Towards the end of 2001—while France was conceding that its own law enforcement policies needed revision, yet turning up its nose at that pathetic "American model"—we witnessed, throughout the nation, marches and demonstrations by police officers and gendarmes who were tired of being increasingly denied the necessary means to fight against civil violence. At the same time, a new law (one that, fortunately, was later revised) on presumption of innocence caused magistrates to release criminals every day, even though they had been arrested *in flagrante delicto*. Such a depressing picture should inspire humility in the French and lead them to draw lessons from the less disastrous experiences of another country rather than launch into tirades against it.

Libération, 22 December 2001. Note that the above three press extracts are spread over a very brief period of time.

But then, why should delinquents and criminals, whether in schools or on the streets, respect the law when encouragement to violate it is trumpeted by the political elites themselves? For example, some leading lights in politics and the media leapt to the aid of the illustrious José Bové, head of the Farmers' Confederation, when in December 2001 he was condemned on appeal to six months in prison for having, along with his hangers-on, destroyed a field of genetically altered rice. Noël Mamère, a *député* and official Green candidate for the presidency of the Republic, declared himself "revolted," adding, "It's a political decision: the real vandals and the real hooligans are Monsanto, Aventis and all the multinationals who, for the sake of their self-interest and profit, want to impose environmental and health risks on people against their will. I denounce this political tribunal, this subversion of justice by the economic lobbies and liberal globalization." Likewise, the spokesman for the Communists claimed to be "scandalized" and asserted that "The war that Bové is waging is an intellectual one."

I won't dwell on the intellectual poverty of these clichés, or the scientific incompetence of the windbags who spout them, or the typical twisting of facts, since the transgenic rice in question was not cultivated by a multinational corporation, but in an experimental field by the National Center for Scientific Research. I *will* point out that here, elected representatives, legislators, indeed candidates for the highest office— which itself is the guarantor of republican institutions—challenged a court decision as being politically manipulated and loudly asserted that criminal acts, punishable in the penal code, are legitimate means of ideological debate in a constitutional democracy. Indoctrinated by public servants of this stripe, our secondary school kids haven't the slightest reason to think they are transgressing the law when they bully other students out of their pocket money, break a chair over the head of a schoolmate, or thrust a knife into a teacher's throat.

Another French failure that has contributed to the growth in urban violence (and rural violence as well, since the explosion of vehicle theft has given greater mobility to criminals) is the failure of integration. This disaster derives partly from the misguided notion of teaching that has prevailed over the last thirty years of the twentieth century, years that witnessed the last spasm of ideology. The ill effects of the notion in question are aggravated by the educational bureaucrats' fear of seeming racist in providing special classes for immigrant students—or the children of immigrants—for whom French is not a native language or an everyday means of communication, at least as they begin school. The pretext for this pedagogical absurdity is to avoid any discrimination against other students. And thanks to such policies, the justifiably feared discrimination has been institutionalized, as North African and other African students, lacking an essential grounding in the language, are condemned to a predictable and virtually permanent failure in school. This sort of failure, promoted by the pedagogues and their political allies, has continued to supply recruits to the delinquent gangs that haunt the neighborhoods. And then, a second hypocrisy, there is a refusal to admit what all serious surveys have established: adolescent violence comes above all from second-generation African immigrants, whose cultural integration has been stymied by a senseless educational policy. The fear of being accused of racism has led politicians to dance away from the issue of ethnic origins when it comes to the street wars.

The writer Christian Jelen has already discussed all this in his book *Les Guerres des rues* ("Wars in the Streets"), published in France in 1998. To say these things openly then was considered scandalous. It required courage of a kind that Jelen, among only a few, displayed. His reasons were quite different from those of right-wing extremists, for he was himself the son of Jewish-Polish immigrants. Three years later, with the spread of a phenomenon that Jelen saw becoming more and more troublesome, the taboo was dropped by the Left as well.

In December 2001, *Le Monde* published a full-page interview with Father Christian Delorme, a priest responsible for community relations with Muslims in the Diocese of Lyon, who over a period of twenty years had favored policies tending to respect and even reinforce Arab-Muslim cultural identity. Father Delorme, whose generous intentions are indisputable, had even created associations of young people that emphasized this ethnic autonomy. By 2001 he recognized that he had been mistaken, and he deplored "a disturbing ethnicizing of social relations." He added: "In France we can't bring ourselves to say certain things, sometimes for laudable reasons. What we've seen for a long time now is the denial of the *superdelinquency of immigrants' offspring*. . . . And still, politicians don't know how to talk about it."* Yet despite his intellectual candor, Father Delorme cannot refrain from projecting this French scourge back onto

---

*_Le Monde,_ 4 December 2001. The italicized phrase was used by _Le Monde_ as the title for the interview.

the United States: "We should denounce the tragedy of ethnic ghettoes, which are becoming, as in the United States, places where resistance to the dominant social model is fomented."

■ ■ ■

BEFORE DISCUSSING THE ISSUE of *communautarisme* (ethnic communities) in America, I would like to mention another example of the European mania for making the United States the cradle of their own problems.

On December 25, 2001, on France Inter Radio, two of the station's special correspondents in Afghanistan reported what they had seen after the rout of the Taliban. Their insights were revealing, as were their conversations with Afghan men and women. Then the journalist hosting the broadcast, who was interviewing the correspondents from Paris, put a closing question to them about the *"imperium"* of American journalists.* Immediately our special correspondents lashed out against American television networks, and CNN in particular, whose newspeople, they said, arrived "with their pockets full of dollars" and thus could rent helicopters and hire better interpreters, among other abuses. And all this expense for what? Almost exclusively in the cause of pro-American propaganda. For example, they contrived to put words into Afghans' mouths expressing happiness at having seen the Taliban chased out of Kabul with the help of American soldiers.

Here we find some of the traditional French obsessions: In the first place, according to these France Inter journalists, who are obviously intelligent and competent, the apparent prowess of the American television networks is due only to the power of money (that uniquely American demon). The Americans' success never owes simply to the talent or professionalism of their journalists, and anyway, what those journalists do is create propaganda, not provide information. It goes without saying among the European elite that for a century or more the American news media have never evidenced the slightest commitment to the ideal of disinterested information or any concern for truth in reportage, and that they are subservient in their editorials to the political powers that be. Delicious critiques coming from a country like France, where for a long

---

*The word *imperium* has no relevance in this context, for in Latin it means the powers of state, comprising military command and legal jurisdiction—powers of a sort that, obviously, no journalist, American or otherwise, can wield. But *imperium* has the advantage of suggesting "imperialism."

time television and radio (including France Inter) were entirely controlled by the government, and where in large part they remain that way.

To return to Father Delorme—whose moderate tone makes his pronouncements all the more telling—he has remarked that "a Pakistani in Great Britain or an Italian in the United States is constantly sent back into his ethnic community." Coming from an informed intellectual, this confusion between the mentality of Anglo-Pakistanis—strident Islamists, the first people to have staged massive demonstrations in 1989 calling for the assassination of Salman Rushdie, even before the *fatwa* of the Ayatollah Khomeini—and that of Italian-Americans gives us pause; we must wonder if ecclesiastical life leaves enough time to read serious books occasionally.

A common refrain in France is: When it comes to immigration, the United States practices *communautarisme*—identity politics and multiculturalism—whereas the French republican tradition has integration as its guiding principle. (If I take so many of my examples from France, it is because France, in my eyes, is the laboratory where one can find in the most extreme and transparent form a set of ideas about the United States that are encountered, in less polemical and more diluted form, throughout Europe and elsewhere.) It is true that the term "community" is often used in the United States, not only in its ethnic or religious sense, but in a vague and general way to denote a city, a neighborhood, a county, an association, a profession, players or fans of a certain sport or almost any activity under the sun. In the ethnic sense of the word, "community" includes customs, beliefs, festivals, cuisine, dress and so on, citizens who are descended from a particular group of immigrants, or immigrants themselves. But this faithfulness to origins should not mislead us. It implies no antagonism between these cultural groups and other American citizens. The Irish community puts on a huge and noisy display in the streets of New York and Boston on St. Patrick's Day, yet these festivities don't prevent the descendants of Irish who arrived in the nineteenth century from feeling fully American—just as the French of the "Aveyronnais de Paris" or the "Francs-Comtois de Lyon" feel themselves to be fully French.*

---

* *Translator's note:* That is, people who have migrated to big cities from rural and mountainous regions such as the Aveyron and the Franche-Comté.

During the last third of the twentieth century, however, a "progressive" elite preached multiculturalism and the right of each ethnic community to assert its "identity"; traditional Americanization was considered oppressive. But by 2002 the multiculturalist project had fallen on hard times, according to the most recent sociological studies. Let me cite one of the best of them: Michael Barone's *The New Americans: How the Melting Pot Can Work Again.** Barone draws interesting parallels between the waves of immigrants in the second half of the nineteenth century and the first third of the twentieth—mainly Irish, Italians and Jews—and arrivals since World War II: blacks, Latinos and Asians. It is surprising to find included in the latter group African-Americans, whose ancestors have been in the United States for at least two centuries, even if against their will. But what Barone describes is the immense migration of blacks from the South to the North after 1945, probably one of the greatest voluntary displacements of a population within one country in history. From 1945 to 1960, at least half of blacks from the Deep South, and notably most of the youth, went to live in the northeastern states. For example, the black population in Chicago went from 278,000 inhabitants in 1940 to 813,000 in 1960; in New York, during the same period of roughly twenty years, it went from 458,000 to 1,088,000. The troubles and feelings of alienation experienced by this population as they struggled to integrate were therefore quite comparable to those experienced by foreign immigrants, given the distance and the cultural abyss that separated the South from the North. Barone shows in convincing fashion that the problems of these blacks and their ways of getting by closely resembled those of the Irish between 1850 and 1914. If one objects that blacks were victims of racial discrimination (though perhaps less so in the North than in the South), Barone replies that the Irish also suffered from discrimination in the early years. Accordingly, the integration of blacks in the northern states reproduced in many respects the experience of the Irish.

The parallels drawn between Jews in the past and Asians today, between Italians in the twentieth century and Latinos in the twenty-first, support Barone's central thesis, which is the continuation and reinvigoration of the melting pot to the detriment of multicultural identity pol-

*Washington, D.C.: Regnery Publishing, 2001.

itics—whatever the prejudices of poorly informed Europeans who persist in taking multiculturalism to be the "American model" par excellence.

One of the last battles of the American "liberal" elite (the French would say "progressive") in favor of ethnic separatism and multicultural identity politics was waged—and lost—over the issue of bilingual education for Latino children in California. In theory, it was about using both Spanish and English in classroom instruction. But in practice, parents saw that their children, speaking Spanish both at home and in school, could learn English only in piecemeal fashion, just enough for small daily transactions and low-wage jobs, but not enough to get a real education, well-paid jobs, or a chance to continue on to university and the professions. This was all the more harmful to them in that their Spanish—the Spanish of families for the most part poor and often illiterate, from Mexico and Central America—was also quite rudimentary. Enclosed in the immigrant milieu by Spanish monolingualism, these young people could not surmount their disadvantages without an opportunity to learn good English in class.

What successful children of immigrants consistently stress is that they succeeded in their studies and in life thanks to pedagogical principles that were totally opposed to those of the pseudo-progressive multiculturalists. This is the story told by Norman Podhoretz in his memoir *My Love Affair with America.** Born in 1930, raised in Brooklyn in a poor Jewish family with roots in Galicia (a province that was continually being exchanged between Poland and the Ukraine), Podhoretz spoke only Yiddish, the language he heard in his home and neighborhood. From the moment that he was old enough to attend school, he began to master English, the only language taught at that time in the American public school system. But still he didn't manage to get rid of his Yiddish accent. So his schoolmistress placed him in a remedial speech class. "Apparently the end result," he writes, "was to eradicate all traces of my Yiddish accent but without putting a Brooklyn accent in its place."

Podhoretz trenchantly sums up the lesson he learned from his experience:

> Because of bilingualism—the demented and discredited theory that the best way to reach English to children from homes in which Spanish or

---

*San Francisco: Encounter Books, 2002.

Chinese or some other language is spoken is to conduct their classes in those other languages—many millions who came or were born here in the last decades of the twentieth century were subjected to the opposite experience from mine. Instead of being helped to share in their inheritance as Americans, they were beset by obstacles blocking their path to it. As I was blessed, so they were cursed, and as I was enriched, so they were impoverished.

In France, on the other hand, the politics of diversity—often called *à l'américaine* but more properly termed *à la française*—has continued its rampage over the past two decades. It is not hard to imagine the cries of indignation that would greet any proposal to give remedial speech therapy to young North Africans and Africans (like the traditional practice in America) that remedied not only the students' accents but also their knowledge and handling of the language, written and spoken. It goes without saying that genuine bilingualism is a blessing, not a curse; but many young "Beurs"* who finish their adolescence in academic failure—to employ the euphemism that disguises the result of stupid educational theories as a sort of natural disaster—don't know Arabic any better than they know French. Unable to participate in the societies to which these languages are the keys, they are culturally marginalized. Perhaps they have gleaned a few scraps of a North African language at home, or learned by heart at the mosque some verses of the Qur'an in classical Arabic, without understanding them; but these linguistic bits and pieces in no way constitute an initiation into Arab culture and thought, and as a result many of our Beurs remain functional illiterates cut off from any real culture, whether ancient or modern, Islamic or European. During the last three decades of the twentieth century, there emerged a destructive "community" politics, a rejectionist multiculturalism that had previously been unknown in France. It was given a powerful impetus as politicians and the media began referring to Jewish, Muslim or Protestant "communities," whereas before there had been citizens or foreign residents of Jewish, Muslim or Protestant confession or tradition. Among all these new communities, the Muslim one is by far the most favored by the authorities. It is

---

* *Translator's note:* "Beur" is a term used to refer to second-generation North African immigrants. It is not considered offensive, and comes from the street *verlan* slang that reverses syllables; thus "Beur" is an inversion of "Arabe." *Verlan* is derived from *"à l'envers,"* or "back to front."

indirectly subsidized, and tacitly if not officially authorized to contravene the law (in the case, for instance, of polygamy).*

But this official deference of the Republic to Muslim cultural and religious "exceptionalism" has done nothing to help integration. On the contrary, it has nourished a hatred without limits, avowed by the children of Muslim immigrants against other French people, whom they resist calling their compatriots. The vast majority of these Beurs could write—if they knew how to write—a book that would be the exact opposite of Norman Podhoretz's and take as its title *My Hate Affair with France.*

This unnecessary state of affairs is largely the product of an educational ideology that, on the pretext of honoring minority identity and promoting egalitarianism, has denied North Africans access to French culture, without preventing them from losing their own—except when it comes to cheering Osama bin Laden and Saddam Hussein. And it has resulted in the absolute contempt for the laws of the Republic that so many Beurs share. For them, the rule of law does not exist, and their wish to remain outside the law reveals itself in a strange form of behavior that I have often analyzed and which could be described as a mechanism for reversing responsibility for crime.

When the Beurs commit an offense, perhaps a murder, and then initiate gunfire during which one of their number is felled by a police bullet, they conveniently forget all about what led up to the last event. In their telling, the scenario begins with the police intervention: in cold blood and without cause, the police killed an Arab. On December 27, 2001, for instance, two masked thugs brandishing handguns entered a bank in Neuilly-sur-Marne, near Paris. The employees, fearful of being killed, handed over a considerable sum of money. Coming out of the bank, the gangsters ran into officers from a nearby police station that a bank telephone operator had been able to alert. They began shooting at the police, who returned fire, killing one of them. The dead man was revealed to be a twenty-one-year-old North African with a history of multiple offenses.

---

*See Pierre-Patrick Kaltenbach's *La France, une chance pour l'Islam* (Le Félin, 1991), and his *Tartuffe aux affairs* (Éditions de Paris, 2001), pp. 112–15. The Council of State has even sometimes shown leniency towards polygamy; see Christian Jelen, *La Famille, secret de l'intégration* (Robert Laffont, 1993).

That night in Vitry-sur-Seine, the fallen criminal's place of residence, and for four or five succeeding nights, bands of roving Beurs trashed the city, setting fire to several dozen cars and attacking the police station with rifles and grenades. (The grenades came from the former Yugoslavia, which brought to light the existence of arms trafficking in the neighborhoods, conducted under the nose of an impotent and incompetent French state.) In the rioters' eyes, the police had cold-bloodedly "assassinated" their comrade. In their selective memory and morality, there had been no holdup, no threats to kill the bank tellers, no armed robbery and no attempt to shake off the police by shooting at them. All the criminal acts were blanketed in amnesia. There remained but one fact: the police had killed one of theirs. It would be difficult to push narcissistic victim politics further, as well as ignorance of the law and the art of shrugging off all responsibility for one's own acts.

The French-style policy of favoritism towards a minority has been stretched so far that the authorities find it almost normal that there are several million people living in France who don't consider themselves subject to the laws of the land. I don't need to emphasize how distant this attitude is from the American practice, which requires that those taking citizenship formally swear to respect the laws and institutions of the country they have chosen and that welcomes them.

"Welcome" is, moreover, not an entirely empty word in the United States. The British journalist Jonathan Freedland quotes these words of an official of the Department of Immigration and Naturalization as he presented citizenship papers to sixty-eight immigrants: "This is a great occasion for the United States. It's people like you who have made and will continue to make this country the most successful in history. People like you have given us outstanding cultural contributions and wonderful intellectual benefits.... You are America."*

Indeed, from 1840 to 1924, 35 million immigrants came to the United States, the equivalent of the entire population of France in 1850 or Italy in 1910. Far from diminishing, this flood has only grown in our time: the census of 2001 recorded 281 million inhabitants, an increase of 30 million over the census of 1991, largely due to immigration and twice the projected figure. To maintain that the melting pot no longer works in America is ideology rather than sociological fact.

---

*Jonathan Freedland, *Bring Home the Revolution* (London: Fourth Estate, 1998).

Here I'd like to slip in a parenthetical point—perhaps obvious, but still worth making. If the picture of American society drawn every day by the European press is accurate, then we must believe that those tens of millions of immigrants from all parts of the world, and especially those who came from Europe between 1850 and 1924, were all deluded fools. Otherwise, why did they insist on staying in the American capitalist jungle with all its evils and not return to the lands of peace, plenty and liberty they came from? Lost in a hellish cultural wasteland, why at least didn't they write to their families and relations basking in the paradises of Ukraine, Calabria and Greece warning them not to come to America? And fifty or a hundred years later, why are Vietnamese, Koreans, Chinese, Mexicans, Salvadorans and even Russians so blind as to fall into the same trap? Wouldn't the descendants of earlier immigrants have explained to them that their forebears had found only poverty, insecurity and oppression in America? One can comprehend how the American Dream could have lured the first arrivals. But if the Dream is only a lie, it's hard to see why the pioneers' bitter disappointments didn't dissuade their successors from taking the same path. History gives us examples of other "dreams" that were quickly revealed as hoaxes, causing people to flee rather than integrate. Were the American "melting pot" a mirage of this kind, we would expect to see disillusioned hordes abandoning the U.S.A. for Albania, Slovakia and Nicaragua.

By contrast, are the North African and African immigrants to France better integrated than they might have been in the United States because we gave up on teaching them French? And because our High Council on Integration refused to institute the equivalent of the American Oath of Allegiance—not being so undemocratic as to require our new French citizens to respect the laws of the Republic? The degree to which they consider themselves exempt from such an obligation has exceeded the most pessimistic expectations.

This is not the case with all of our immigrants, thankfully. Throughout our society can be found French citizens of North African and African origin who have successfully integrated morally, politically and professionally; they can be blue-collar workers, office workers, storekeepers, teachers, physicians, lawyers, public-sector employees or civil servants. But we never hear them express themselves as representatives of their "community" at moments of crisis, when their statements might counterbalance the hatred of their brethren. They have been marginalized by the radicals, the urban armed gangs that monopolize "community" representation. Why, exactly?

The politically correct sociologists—really, conformists of the pseudo-Left—assure us that the radicals, who have transformed so many cities into "lawless zones," are but a small minority. If this is the case, why haven't the forces of law and order been able to control them? How is it that, for several years in a row (in Strasbourg and Nantes, for example), rioters could trash entire neighborhoods and burn hundreds of cars with impunity? The answer brings government incompetence into relief, but also the relative isolation of well-integrated immigrants.

Whether described as incompetent or indulgent, the government's inaction amounts to officially sanctioning illegality, just as the lack of discipline or serious instruction at school has virtually been given official sanction. Thus has the criminal "community" been able to take shape, even legitimize itself—which is all the more dangerous in that, while it stridently claims to be discriminated against, it is itself deeply xenophobic and racist. Though their well-publicized "hatred" is directed against the French in general, it is against the Jews that it is most sharply focused: between October 1, 2000, and July 1, 2002, there were numerous anti-Semitic terrorist assaults against synagogues as well as Jewish schools, businesses and even private homes. Evidently, our Muslims like to make their feelings felt as one community set against another, subverting our long republican tradition, which assumes but one national community.* And with that very French administrative art of minimizing crimes they have given up fighting against, the minister of the interior of the moment said dismissively that those assaults were the work of "young people with nothing better to do." Likewise, the Bouches-du-Rhône prefect of police, after the arson of a Jewish school in Marseilles, merely remarked that they were dealing with a "sad social phenomenon."

These spokesmen for what used to be the rule of law sound less like responsible officials than melancholy moralists. They could not have expressed more clearly their unshakeable determination to do nothing. Wasn't the mayor of Strasbourg crowing over a victory when, on January

---

*See *L'Express*, 6 December 2001. In his editorial, Denis Jeambar, the magazine's editor, writes: "It's a fact that these anti-Semitic acts are committed in the main by Muslims."

1, 2002, on the night of Saint Sylvester, "only" 44 cars had been torched, down from 55 the previous year?

In view of this now permanent street warfare, the French are in a poor position to denigrate America's truly diverse, multifaceted society. The success and originality of American integration stems precisely from the fact that immigrants' descendants can perpetuate their ancestral cultures while thinking of themselves as American citizens in the fullest sense. Each community can finance private schools where children, during vacations, may be initiated into Greek, Farsi or Hebrew. Throughout the country, one can tune in to radio stations in Korean, Spanish and many other languages, without implying the slightest conflict with American society at large. After all, these diverse cultural experiences are its source and fulfillment.

It is this harmonious equilibrium between traditions and citizenship that we haven't been able to achieve in France. As soon as the issue of teaching a regional language in one or another of our provinces is raised, the initiative is often resented as a politically motivated attempt to eliminate French. The Qur'anic *madrasahs* and the mosques are not so much schools for the transmission of the Arabic language and Arab culture as centers of anti-French and fundamentalist propaganda.

In the United States, the English language from the beginning played a unifying role that was entirely accepted and even greater than in the United Kingdom itself. "In consequence of the frequent removals of people from one part of our country to another," wrote John Pickering in 1816, "[there is] greater uniformity of dialect throughout the United States ... than is to be found throughout England." Quoting this observation in *The Americans,* Daniel Boorstin notes that the English spoken in the United States, in contrast to the English of the British Isles, quickly became standardized throughout the land, for every social class and in every sociocultural group—Italian, Polish, German, Jewish, Mexican, Chinese and so forth. By way of comparison, in France's 1794 Convention, Abbot Grégoire stated that at least 6 million French (out of a population of 27 million) did not speak the national tongue and that the number of people who spoke a pure French did not exceed 3 million.

The French seem unaware that the melting pot philosophy they berate as *communautarisme à l'américaine* has nevertheless been a factor in their own history. The process by means of which immigrants—of highly varied geographical provenance and significant demographic weight—melt into the culture of their adopted country, while managing to preserve certain traditions of their forebears, has been constant. French people of Orthodox background, descended from Eastern European immigrants, do not feel they are setting themselves up against other French Christians when they celebrate Christmas on January 7 and the New Year on January 13. And French Jews, by observing their New Year in September or October, do not consider themselves on this account to be second-class citizens and culturally less French than their compatriots. Compatibility between the general and the particular, between full membership in the larger society and maintenance of religious practices, distinctive folk customs, traditional clothing and culinary savoir-faire: this is what characterizes not only the American civilization, but the process of evolution and enlightenment in almost all the great civilizations.

The French leftist and politically correct "associations," even government authorities, maintain an intrinsically contradictory argument in this area: on the one hand, they hold what they suppose to be American-style ethnic relations in contempt; on the other, they proclaim that some immigrant populations have the right to a "distinctive identity," up to and including illiteracy and polygamy—which ensures that they will be denied the chance to blend in. But conscious, voluntary cultural assimilation is essential if the disasters of unemployment, street warfare and so on are to be avoided. And successful integration itself will only be enriched by further contributions from new cultures. The melding occurs by subtle stages, as the French have experienced frequently in the course of their history.

During the nineteenth and twentieth centuries, France continued to receive diverse waves of Italians, Armenians, Greeks, Poles, Hungarians, Spanish, Portuguese, Jews from Central and Eastern Europe. These groups, fleeing poverty or political persecution or both, were sometimes large enough to transform a region or a town's demographic composition. In 1926, Albert Londres reported that when he heard only Italian spoken around the Old Harbor of Marseilles, he asked the mayor, a certain Flaissière, "Tell me, what city are you the mayor of?" Flaissière retorted: "Come on, you're still only half awake this morning. I'm the mayor of Naples, of course!"* The children of these Italians, or Armenians, or (in the north

---

*Albert Londres, *Marseilles, porte du Sud;* quoted by Christian Jelen in *La Famille, secret de l'intégration* (Robert Laffont, 1993).

of France) Poles were nonetheless to become fully integrated, just as were the Spanish and Portuguese after World War II; yet all could retain a strong attachment to their parents' culture. The life of filmmaker Henri Verneuil, who died in January 2002, illustrates this.

Verneuil's films are among the most "French" of the French cinema. Yet his real name was Achod Malakian, and he was the son of Armenian parents, survivors of genocide, who arrived in Marseilles when he was four years old. He was of course as perfectly at home with the French language as any other Marseillais, but he never gave up speaking fluent Armenian as well. He always liked to point out this fusion of Frenchman and Armenian within himself. So the radical opposition made between integration and minority cultural identity is erroneous, or at least needs to be qualified. But what has happened during the last quarter of the twentieth century is that the two have come to be regarded as mutually exclusive. The question is: why?

Why is the characteristic attitude of North African, African and Turkish immigrant groups, which by the second generation largely consist of French nationals, so predominantly one of alienation, confrontation, rejection, hatred?

In his book *La Famille, secret de l'intégration,* Christian Jelen brings together some of the factors that point to the answer. Former immigrants, even the poorest, were for the most part able to assimilate successfully for two essential reasons: the respect given by children to family authority and the unqualified faith in education as the indispensable path to cultural integration in the host country.

We find these social and cultural characteristics as much among the immigrants of former times—Italians, Armenians and Jews—as among later newcomers and those of today who assimilate smoothly: Portuguese, Vietnamese and Chinese. On the other hand, we find these formative assets hardly at all among North African immigrants and even less among those from sub-Saharan Africa. Among the latter, failure is exacerbated by polygamy. This is a custom that our political leaders, through politically correct hypocrisy, refrain from mentioning at all costs yet discreetly allow, in defiance of the laws of the Republic. The word "polygamy" is "banished from every report and commentary," adds Jelen, who devotes a chapter to this phenomenon and its baleful consequences.

Parental irresponsibility, which allows youth to spend their time haunting the streets in gangs, is the principal cause of neighborhood degradation, the spread of violent disorder and the inevitable slide of young people—even children—into delinquency and crime. Municipal authorities have tried to do something about parental dereliction of duty, proposing either to reduce the state-paid benefits to parents guilty of neglect, or to impose a curfew that would make children under twelve or thirteen years of age (indeed, much less than that, but how can any-one prove this when they have no identity papers?) return home before midnight. And for this they have been called fascists and racists by the parties, officials and journalists of the Left, which has been hard at work destroying one of the necessary conditions for assimilation.

The second necessary condition, success in school, has been under-mined by the pedagogical theories—or rather, antipedagogical theories—deriving from the ideologies of 1968, which also began to be put into practice over the last quarter of the century. The deleterious effect that these have had for every category of student is naturally most severe for the children of immigrants, who have the biggest obstacles to surmount. For most of them, the application of these theories was the coup de grâce, to which was added North African and African parents' incomprehen-sion of the importance of regular attendance at school. Examples of this are legion; how many letters to parents there must have been from pri-mary and secondary school teachers, pointing out persistent absences and suggesting face-to-face talks about such problems—only to remain unan-swered. Yet if educators so much as assign low grades to students or attempt calling them to order, they risk getting their faces smashed in or being knifed. In 1950, immigrant parents would invariably be on the side of a primary school teacher who wanted to make her charges work and do well on tests. From around 1975 to 1980, they have been against her.

So it's hard to see how the integration of these recent immigrants could succeed when even the public officials of the host country appear to be against it, since they refrain from encouraging the newcomers to develop the necessary good habits. This is how, since 1970, the new French ideology has made up out of whole cloth a fraudulent notion of "com-munity," hitherto entirely unknown in France, that is labeled "Ameri-can" the better to exonerate its architects from culpability and to feign forgetfulness that what we have today is well and truly a French creation. It is yet another example of passing the buck, of dodging responsibility, of projecting one's own faults onto another, that is a basic function of anti-Americanism.

Let me point out one further contradiction, going back to the nineteenth century: Europeans alternately describe American society as a mass of rootless, isolated individuals struggling against each other in Darwinian competition, or as a conformist, easily led herd, where the individual can neither think nor act for himself.

5. Cultural Extinction

"CULTURAL DIVERSITY" HAS REPLACED "cultural exceptionalism" in the French-inspired, European rhetoric. But in actuality, the two terms cover the same kind of cultural protectionism. The idea that a culture can preserve its originality by barricading itself against foreign influences is an old illusion that has always produced the opposite of the desired result. Isolation breeds sterility. It is the free circulation of cultural products and talents that allows each society to perpetuate and renew itself.

The proof of this goes back to the old comparison between Athens and Sparta. It was Athens, the open city, that was prolifically creative in letters and arts, philosophy and mathematics, political science and history. Sparta, jealously guarding its "exceptionalism," pulled off that tour de force of being the only Greek city not to have produced a single notable poet, orator, thinker or architect; their achievement was "diversity" of a sort, but at the price of emptiness. Parallel phenomena of cultural vacuity are found again in contemporary totalitarian states. Fear of ideological contamination induced the Nazis, the Soviets and the Maoists to take refuge in an "official" art and a pompously dogmatic literature, sheer insults to the heritage of the peoples on whom they were inflicted.

When Jean-Marie Messier, in December 2001, said that "French cultural exceptionalism is dead," he aroused horrified protests, but he was not going nearly far enough. He could have added: in fact, French cultural exceptionalism has never existed, thank goodness. If it had, it would be French culture itself that would be extinct. Let's suppose that the sixteenth-century kings of France, instead of inviting Italian artists to their courts, had said to themselves: "This predominance of Italian painting is insufferable. We'll keep those Italians and their pictures out of the country." The result of this démarche would have been to thwart a renewal of French art. Again: between 1880 and 1914 there were many more French Impressionist paintings in American museums and the homes of private collectors than there were in France; despite which—or because of which—American art was subsequently able to find its own inspiration, and then influence French art in turn.

These cross-fertilizations are indifferent to political antagonisms. It was during the first half of the seventeenth century, when France and Spain were frequently at war, that the creative influence of Spanish literature on the French was particularly marked. The eighteenth century, which saw repeated conflict between France and England, was also the period when the most active and productive intellectual exchanges between the two countries occurred. And between 1870 and 1945, diplomatic relations between France and Germany were hardly idyllic, yet these were the years when German philosophers and historians had the most to teach the French. And wasn't Nietzsche steeped in the ideas of the French moralists? It would be possible to extend indefinitely the list of examples illustrating this truth: cultural diversity arises from manifold exchanges. This applies just as well to gastronomy: only McDonald's-hating lunatics are unaware of the obvious fact that there have never been so many restaurants offering foreign cuisines, in practically every country, as in our day. Far from imposing standardization, international exchange diversifies. Withdrawing behind a wall can only dry up inspiration.

In practice, Europeans—and chiefly the French—use the jargon phrases "cultural exceptionalism" and "cultural diversity" as code words for state aid and quotas. We keep hearing from the protectionists that, after all, "Cultural goods are not simple commodities." But that is merely a platitude. Whoever pretended that they were? Still, neither are they simply the products of state financing; otherwise, Soviet painting would have been the finest in the world. Those who advocate protecting the arts against market forces, while they insist on supporting them with subsidies, are guilty of self-contradiction. "Don't make such a fuss over money for the arts!" they chide condescendingly, stressing the need to fund artistic creation—but it seems that only taxpayers' money will do. Granted, talented creators may sometimes be in need of financial assistance, but this doesn't mean that money can make talent.

"Look at the Italian film industry," people say. "Without government support, it has practically disappeared." Yet in the years after the war, the brilliance of Italian cinema came not from subsidies, but from Rossellini and De Sica, Blasetti and Castellani, Visconti and Fellini. Similarly, Spanish cinema owed its blossoming in the 1980s to the imagination of its creators and not to ministerial grants. And if the French film industry today has recaptured market leadership at home and found successes abroad, this is not because it is more subsidized than formerly, but because it has managed to produce a handful of films whose quality was appreciated not only by their *auteurs,* but by the public. A commercially successful French cinema with international appeal displays a more authentic diversity than the kind preached by tiresome diversity-mongers.

This revival must be placed in perspective, however. As Dominique Moïsi had the audacity to write, "The irony of this debate is increased by the fact that last year, the symbol of France's successful resistance to Hollywood's hegemony was a pleasant but very superficial comedy, *Le Fabuleux Destin d'Amélie Poulain* ["Amélie"], a string of trendy clips in advertising style without any social or intellectual content whatsoever. By comparison, Ken Loach's penetrating films, which owe nothing to cultural exceptionalism, reflect a stimulating, refreshing cultural diversity."* And Moïsi lamented that instead of the serious discussion that the whole question of state support (or favoritism) versus the public's market choice deserves, we have "a frenzied defense of the universal nature of the French exception."

You don't have to be an Aristotle or a Leibniz to grasp that "universal exceptionalism" is a contradiction in terms on the most elementary level of logic. And it is not the only such contradiction in a confused quarrel that has more to do with strong emotions than rational analysis. So Denis Olivennes, who heads Canal +, a television network that plays a big role in the financing of the French film industry, argues that a linchpin of this support is a tax on all new releases. In this way, he writes, "American films, which represent about half of new releases, contribute half of the funding." Here is impressive sleight of hand. For it's obvious that the money does not come from American films, but rather from

---

*"Les Deux Frances," *Les Echos,* 14 January 2002. It's worth pointing out, however, that the French film industry's two big hits in 2001–2002, *Le Fabuleux Destin d'Amélie Poulain* and *Astérix et Obélix: Mission Cléopâtre,* were shot in German and English studios. The reason for this is that the French government robs successful producers in order to subsidize hacks.

French filmgoers. More generally, the opposition between the state and the market in relation to the arts, between public moneys and the money of the public, is a misleading one. Public funds have but one source: the public, which is taxed by one means or another, directly or indirectly. The question is what portion of the public's contribution is freely offered and what portion is milked from it by government fiat, then spent according to the whims of a minority of political and administrative decision-makers and commissions whose members are appointed, not elected.

A culture becomes decadent when it takes to running down other cultures while heaping praises on itself. Thus the professionals of radio and television keep harping on the notion—which they end up seeming to believe and making their audiences believe—that American television movies, produced with the sole aim of making a profit, avoid all controversial social and political issues. But French series, we are told over and over again, draw from a tradition of publicly funded state television; even productions from our privatized networks follow the aesthetic canons of this tradition. So they escape the "tyranny of profit" and can risk upsetting some of their viewers by courageously airing serious, painful controversies.

Actually, the opposite is true. Michel Winkler has given ample proof of this in his *Mirrors of Life,* about American television series. In an interview on Monde television, Winkler (a physician and a novelist) said: "French television series are not designed to make you think. The three main networks have one and the same policy when it comes to TV drama: . . . catering to conformism. The viewers are treated like sheep." In the United States, conversely, "television, with its social critiques, has taken over from the cinema of the years between 1930 and 1950." Conventional French productions hold the public all the more captive in that only 15 percent of French people have access to cable or satellite TV, compared with 80 percent of Americans.

As an example, consider the episodic television drama about the Watergate affair that was filmed and broadcast in the U.S. very soon after Richard Nixon's resignation in the mid-sixties. The actor who played the president was virtually his double, and all the others were easily identifiable as real characters. And of course this was not the only national scandal that would furnish the plot for an American TV production or movie, or a scenario close to actual events. But I'm still waiting for French equivalents: exposés, perhaps, of the insider trading that led to Pechiney's buyout of Triangle—insiders, it seems, at the highest levels of government—and of the Crédit Lyonnais and Elf scandals. If they were to be comparable to American productions, they would have to be accurate renditions of these episodes, highly unflattering to France, with a cast closely modeled on the original. It's likely that we'll have to wait a long time for these programs.

Rehashing one of the stalest Marxist clichés, Catherine Tasca, the French minister of culture, told *Figaro Magazine* that "market laws are the totems of American power." In fact, market laws are not so much totems as explanation.

■ ■ ■

IN THE CULTURAL AS in other domains, the quarrel with globalization that flared up during the 1990s actually represents a resistance to Americanization. Here again, in our perception of America's influence as a threat and a disease, we should distinguish between what is fantastical and what is justified. And we should ask ourselves if American culture might include achievements and ways of doing things that others would do well to look at and emulate.

The fear of seeing cultural identities drowned in a kind of planetary standardization, which today is thought to be overwhelmingly American in coloration but in former times showed other hues, has no basis in historical fact or impartial observation of today's reality. The commingling of cultures, with predominance going first to one and then to another, has always led—in antiquity, in the medieval period and in the modern world—not to uniformity, but to diversity. This is what is happening today, as the Swedish essayist Johan Norberg (among many others) has pointed out:

> Many people are afraid that the world will become McDonaldized and homogenized: we will all end up wearing the same clothes, seeing the same films. But this is not a good description of the globalization process. Take a walk in Stockholm and look for yourself. Of course you'll find burgers and Coca Cola, but you can also pick and choose from shish kebab, sushi, Tex-Mex, Peking duck, French cheeses, Thai soup.

And the author recalls what is frequently forgotten: that American culture is not just songs by Madonna and action films starring Arnold Schwarzenegger; it includes 1,700 symphony orchestras, opera attended by 7.5 million people every year, and museums that are visited by 500

109

million annually. Almost all American museums, where entrance is quite often free, owe their existence and funding to private sponsors.

It is surprising that artists should have so little esteem for their art that they regard its international dissemination as strictly dependent on the power of money and advertising. Bertrand Tavernier, for example, whom I nevertheless knew to be a connoisseur of American cinema before he became a filmmaker, explained its success in these terms: "With the complicity of certain politicians and even newspapers . . . relying on a bomb-proof distribution system, Americans impose their films on us."* Yet Tavernier ought to know that a work of literature or art, and especially a work of entertainment, can never be imposed on the public by force or cajoling. All the coercive power of the Soviet Union never succeeded, however much the commissars might have wanted to, in "imposing" official literature on readers, who preferred the clandestinely circulated, mimeographed material famously known as "samizdat" (literally, "self-published"). When the authors or distributors of this literature were caught by the police, they were charged with "cosmopolitanism"—another name for globalism—and sent to prison camps or special psychiatric hospitals.

In January 2002, when Yves Saint Laurent unexpectedly announced his decision to retire, suddenly bringing his career as couturier to an end, reaction to the news was worldwide. And it was not only Saint Laurent's talent that was influential everywhere, but also that of his predecessors, who for over a century had created and sustained French leadership in haute couture (which is not to diminish the excellence of other schools, notably the Italian). There was no suggestion in the foreign press that this traditional preeminence of French haute couture or Saint Laurent's influence was attributable to a "bomb-proof distribution system" that, with the shady complicity of "politicians and newspapers," had succeeded in "imposing" French styles on others. Anyone who said as much would have been ridiculed.

But the French make themselves liable to such ridicule when they assess the achievements of others. For instance, between 1948 and 1962, the majority of top prizes at the Venice Biennales were conferred on artists of the Paris school. But in 1964, when the first prize was awarded to Robert Rauschenberg, the newest leading light of a New York school that

---

*Quoted in Mario Roy's *Pour en finir avec l'antiaméricanisme* (Québec: Éditions du Boréal, 1993). Must one suppose, then, that our own distribution system is susceptible to bombing?

had been showing great vitality for twenty years, the French cried scandal, imperialism and collusion with dealers. Some of our officials accused the U.S. government of pressuring the Italian government and made other extravagant claims that didn't show them at their finest.

Giancarlo Pajetta, an important Italian Communist leader, once said, "I finally understand what pluralism is: it's when lots of people share my point of view." In that spirit, governments and elites almost everywhere have signed on to cultural globalism, provided that their own countries are its source and model. In 1984, presenting a *Projet culturel extérieur de la France,* the French government said, with signal modesty, that this manifesto had "no parallel in other countries." All cultures are of equal value, conceded the authors of this official document (a statement erring on the side of simplistic political correctness), but *our* culture is predestined to be a universal mediator, for it is "shared by people of every continent." Touching optimism indeed, which naturally led up to the conclusion that "the future of the French language in the world can only be as a promoter of cultural progress and is closely linked to the future of people everywhere." Global homogenization of culture, in the illusions of these authors, is fine—provided that it emanates from France.

And the homogenization in question, which today is perceived most often as Americanization, is (insofar as it exists) American only in its most superficial and least durable aspects. It is above all the vehicle for popular culture—the entertainments, clothing styles and fast foods favored by the young, and popular music (but not all of it, by any means). Here the word "culture" is being used in the rather loose sense that has prevailed because it is the entertainment industry that leads the choir in lamenting American influence. This influence may present a problem, but to identify the whole of cultural life with entertainment is a travesty.

Whether the film industry people like it or not, culture also includes literature, science, architecture and painting. Let's face the facts: American novelists most influenced European writing between the World Wars, at a time when the United States was not yet considered the world's greatest power—a status that was most often accorded to Great Britain. After the Second World War, when the United States became politically dominant, Latin American literature achieved a success in Europe, both with the critics and with the public, exceeding North America's, although the latter could boast talents of the first order during this period also. As Mario Vargas Llosa wrote in October 2000:

ANTI-AMERICANISM

> Barely fifty years ago we Spanish speakers formed a community that was closed in on itself, hardly venturing outside our linguistic borders. Today, on the other hand, the Spanish language is showing a growing vitality and tends to be gaining bridgeheads and sometimes strong positions on all five continents. The fact that today there are 20 to 30 million Spanish speakers in the United States explains why the two candidates for the presidency, Governor Bush and Al Gore, make use of Spanish on the campaign trail.*

Here is yet another example of globalization enhancing cultural diversity, in the United States as elsewhere.

I should also mention the international audience for Japanese literature in the second half of the twentieth century, and the slow but irresistible rise to literary preeminence of a writer like V. S. Naipaul, winner of the Nobel Prize in 2001, whose cultural roots are multiple and complex: West Indian, Indian and English, but in any case not American. Likewise, French dramatists have been much more conspicuous internationally than North Americans; and the Italian poets Ungaretti and Montale are more famous than their American counterparts.

I am reluctant to extend this list of textbook banalities, but one must attempt somehow to counter somehow the overblown and hypocritical alarums over threats to cultural diversity. The fact is that diversity has never been greater. Obviously, globalization since 1945 has permitted an ever-freer circulation of intellectual goods throughout the world, accompanied by an ever-growing number of aesthetic styles. How many French authors were translated into Japanese in the nineteenth century, and vice versa? Today, almost all of them are.

I am not aware that Italian, Scandinavian, South American, French, Swiss and other architects receive fewer commissions than their North American counterparts. All these nationalities and many others have supplied and continue to supply stellar names to architecture, and their creative genius, without loss of originality, has been stimulated by interaction; here again, diversity has been a beneficiary. As for painting, if the emergence of the New York school around 1960 caused French painters and critics, accustomed to a position of dominance for two centuries, to gnash their teeth, it is difficult to deny that it had a diversifying rather than a

---

*"Cultures locales et mondialisation," *Commentire,* Autumn 2000.

112

homogenizing effect. The same is true for the Cobra group in northern Europe and the Italian renewal around the same time.

Contrary to what Jacques Chirac maintained, globalization is not a "cultural steamroller."* It is and always has been an engine of enrichment. Think, for example, how the French artistic sensibility was revitalized by the discovery—or rather, a fuller knowledge—of Japanese painting at the end of the nineteenth century, and by the arrival in France of African art ten or twenty years later. There are plenty of similar cases. Unless one has been brainwashed by the brawlers of Seattle and Porto Alegre, the age-old lesson of civilization cannot be erased: barriers are what diminish and sterilize cultures, whereas commingling is what fructifies and inspires them.

Science is a different matter. Research depends much more on financial support than do other pursuits. This fact partly explains the current American dominance, but only partly. It also stems from the way that American universities manage to combine teaching and research much more closely than their European counterparts, excepting German and British institutions. This is one of the reasons why American universities attract so many foreign students and professors. In its report for 2002, the French revenue court criticized—yet again—the CNRS (Centre National de la Recherche Scientifique) for its sclerosis, aging scientists and absence of peer revue. This pessimistic diagnosis is a refrain that has been periodically repeated over the last few decades; but, as is common in France in every domain, it has never led to the slightest reform. Despite these shortcomings, some Nobel Prizes have gone to French scientists in recent decades, as well as to scientists of other countries, although the United States has won the largest number by far. So geographical diversity still prevails in the sciences, even though the notion of "diversity" in science itself is relatively meaningless: scientific knowledge, in contrast to the understanding of sculpture or music, is no different in Tokyo, Rome or Bombay than it is in Massachusetts or California.

The equal-opportunity nature of scientific knowledge means that internationalism is a necessary condition for its most rapid progress. If Descartes, through philosophical dogmatism, had not rejected Galileo's physics, perhaps it might have fallen to a French scientist to make the

---

*Quoted in *Le Journal du dimanche*, 3 February 2002.

discoveries that Newton eventually made in England, where speculation was much less constrained by metaphysical presuppositions than it was in France. And if Islam had not rejected modern science, perhaps Muslim countries would not have suffered from the "cultural exceptionalism" that has been theirs, and not always helpful, for the last three centuries.

For a culture to be strong and internationally prominent depends on the scope and quality of education at home and within its domain of influence, and how it adapts to evolving knowledge. The deterioration of elementary and secondary teaching in France since about 1970 is an acknowledged catastrophe, abundantly documented and discussed. But there is less agreement about the deficiencies of French universities. At a time when a growing portion of the population has access to higher education, the quality of university instruction is crucial for the health of a culture and its appeal to outside observers.

Why do students, teachers and researchers from every country in the world swarm to American schools and not to ours? In an important study, *L'Université française du xixe au xxie siècle,** Jean-Claude Casanova ruthlessly exposes how French higher education has failed in comparison with what is available in the United States. One reason is a simple lack of money. The author notes that the endowment of Harvard, certainly not the largest university in America, is close to $20 billion—more than twice the annual expenditure of France on its entire university system. A second cause of our weakness stems from the bad idea that, since the beginning of the nineteenth century, has promoted administrative centralization. For a long time we have spoken of "the French university" rather than "French universities." By the late nineteenth century, in his *Les Origines de la France contemporaine,* Hippolyte Taine was convincingly describing the cultural sclerosis engendered by this academic authoritarianism.

To this lack of autonomy in our universities was added the mistake of separating teaching from research. For fifty years the harmful consequences have been regularly denounced by prominent French scientists, above all those who have had experience with German, British and American universities. In this area as elsewhere, French reluctance to take

---

*Published in the series *La France du nouveau siècle,* under the direction of Thierry de Montbrial (PUF, 2002).

account of the most incontrovertible studies and to make reforms (except in rhetorical fashion) has perpetuated this absurd divorce. Finally, a third weakness, according to Casanova, is that "the French university system was slow to extend education to the masses, by contrast with American universities, the first in the world to get serious about this task from the middle of the twentieth century onwards."

True culture always transcends national frontiers. Among all the contradictions of anti-Americanism, one of the oddest is that one finds condemnation of cultural internationalism even when roles are reversed—that is, when it is American culture or popular culture that is subject to foreign influence. Thus, a Quebecois journalist blathers against "the cultural fast food of the hour ... *The Phantom of the Opera,* a cultural equivalent of the Big Mac."* As it happens, the show that Mme. Vaillancourt is talking about was originally not an American but a British production; and journalists should know that it was developed from the renowned French novel that came out in 1910, *Le Fantôme de l'opéra,* which we owe to Gaston Leroux. We ought to be happy that a popular French book finds itself, by way of an American adaptation, translated onto movie screens throughout the world. But in Mario Roy's pertinent comment, "Facts have never been the point, of course."

Hatred of America is sometimes pushed to the point where it transmutes into hatred for ourselves. This is what we saw when the Disneyland near Paris was opened in 1992. This event was denounced by our intellectuals as a "cultural Chernobyl." But you will notice, even without exceptional erudition, that a large part of Walt Disney's themes, especially in his feature movies, are drawn from European sources. *Snow White and the Seven Dwarves, Sleeping Beauty,* Carlo Collodi's *Pinocchio,* the musical scores in *Fantasia,* the reconstruction of the pirate's ship from Robert Louis Stevenson's *Treasure Island*—all are borrowings from, and homages to, European creativity. And Disney pays deference to other traditional masterpieces from various cultures—for example, *The Thousand and One Nights.*

That these popular stories, the flowers of the imagination of so many different peoples over so many centuries, orally transmitted from generation to generation, then collected and fixed in written form, should

---

*Julie Vaillancourt in *Le Devoir,* 22 December 1992, cited by Mario Roy in *Pour en finir avec l'antiaméricanisme.*

finally appear in a completely new medium thanks to the unique talent of a Californian artist—isn't this an example of the unforeseeable paths and crossroads of cultures? Their dynamic motifs travel by varied routes and vehicles, ancient and modern, regardless of the prudish chauvinism of narrow-minded protectionists.

The latter will surely raise the objection that the exploitation of these ancient legends from East and West by American show business can only betray their special qualities by deforming and commercializing them. Hollywood, as everyone knows, or ought to know, has never been anything but the capital of bad taste, vulgarity and banality. American show business destroys other cultures more than it honors them.

But at this point, we have left the sphere of reason to enclose ourselves in self-contradictory fantasies.

Curiously enough, in the countries where we are most likely to hear such trivial diatribes, we often find a suicidal propensity to destroy the domestic cultural patrimony. In his book on the history of cultural despoliation in France, Louis Réau draws up the appalling list of architectural masterpieces that have been demolished, burned down or defaced.* This has occurred in every period, but by a strange irony especially during and after the French Revolution—that is, during the most virulent phase of French cultural nationalism. Bringing Réau's work up to date, Michel Fleury and Guy-Michel Leproux draw a no less dismaying picture of the vandalism committed since 1958, when the Fifth Republic proclaimed a redoubled *politique culturelle de la France* and, under the pretext of modernization, carried out a methodical uglification of Paris, destroying or neglecting precious works of our architectural heritage. Moreover, the law of decentralization, whereby certain powers accrue to local elected officials, has *ipso facto* increased their capacity for provincial vandalism tenfold. We can no longer even count the buildings put up to house municipal, departmental or regional councils on the sites of razed historical monuments, not to mention the old structures that have been "remodeled" to the point of annihilation. In 1990, for example, the city council of Nîmes voted for the demolition of a medieval house decorated with frescos. When one of the councilors—an old-fashioned eccentric—protested against this sacrilege, he

---

*Louis Réau, *Histoire du vandalisme: Les monuments détruits de l'art français* (Robert Laffont, 1994).

was rebutted by the first deputy mayor and the deputy for culture, who peremptorily informed him: "This particular *hôtel* wasn't medieval; it dated from the fourteenth century." To have been so ignorant of how the historical periods are demarcated in France, this pair of philistines must have been Americans, of course!

From 2000 on, this enthusiasm for laying waste to historic landmarks gained the support of the administrative body that was specifically invested with responsibility to preserve and maintain them and open them to the public: the Centre des Monuments Nationaux. In a pseudo-modernist fit, these *fonctionnaires* have decided that the patrimony, such as it is—probably no longer of any intrinsic interest in their eyes—must henceforth pay tribute to the *animation culturelle* ("cultural conversation"), an expression connoting empty and conformist chatter. It is laudable to want to encourage contemporary creativity, but it is hard to understand why this should be contingent upon the obliteration of earlier achievements.

Why, for example, in L'Hôtel de Sully—one of the pearls of the Marais and one of the few seventeenth-century dwellings that have been preserved intact, with its period tapestries designed by Simon Vouet and the gallery of portraits of the Sully family—was the great hall repainted in garish yellow and pink and disfigured with trendy chandeliers that evoke not so much Henri IV or Louis XIII as a palatial Indonesian seaside resort for *nouveaux riches?* By what right did officials, charged with watching over the upkeep of landmarks that the public comes to visit specifically to learn about their cultural heritage, perpetrate such travesties? It's true that the personal cultural level of these people seems to have fallen drastically over the last one or two generations. When the conservator of the Château de Chambord suggested bringing the château into the modern world by putting on a production of Molière's *Le Bourgeois gentilhomme,* an assistant director of Action Culturelle replied, "Apart from *Phèdre,* Molière is boring."*

Clearly, the self-inflicted attack on the French cultural heritage is much more dangerous than the so-called "steamroller" of globalization. And France is certainly not the only country where an autodestructive

---

*Reported in *Le Figaro,* 2–3 February 2002, where Anne-Marie Romero devotes a long and detailed article to the Sully scandal and similar fiascos. (*Phèdre,* of course, is Racine's most famous play.)

frenzy, usually with roots in ideology and ambitions of specious innovation, has been on the loose. It has caused massive and irreparable artistic losses in China under Mao, as Simon Leys dared to document while Mao-worship was pervasive among our chattering classes.*

Shame at seeing the variety of cultures allegedly being effaced for the profit of America alone is reinforced by another factor, this one very real: the international spread of the English language. English is the mother tongue of approximately 380 million human beings. Almost an equal number use it as a second language, not counting the legions who know a few words and phrases, an indispensable minimum of the lingua franca for travel abroad, even in non-Anglophone countries. If this internationalization of English increasingly results from American superpower, does that mean it must lead to the cultural Americanization of the planet? Not at all. Obviously, learning enough English for everyday needs—for commercial exchanges, financial transactions, even political and diplomatic business—doesn't require even a superficial familiarity with Anglo-American culture and thought, much less the abandonment of one's own culture. The utilitarian use of English by hundreds of millions of our contemporaries is clearly not incompatible with a total ignorance of the great writers and thinkers as well as the historical, political and religious events that have forged the British and American civilizations. Conversely, someone who knows scarcely a word of the Russian language can be imbued with the Russian sensibility thanks to assiduous reading of Russian classics in the often fine translations that have been made in so many languages.

And then, globalization is equally a factor in the learning of foreign languages other than English. As Mario Vargas Llosa writes, "How many millions of young people of both sexes, throughout the world, have undertaken, thanks to globalization, to learn Japanese, German, Mandarin and Cantonese Chinese, Arabic, Russian or French? Undoubtedly the number is very large, and this is a sign of our times; the trend, fortunately, will continue to grow in years to come."** So let's not forget: globalization is really the facilitation of travel, both mentally and physically. The

---

*See my *Images brisées* (Robert Laffont, 1976) and *Ombres chinoises* (Robert Laffont, 1978).
**"Cultures locales et mondialisation," *Commentaire,* Autumn 2000.

farthest destinations, once accessible only to the wealthy, are now within reach of a vast crowd of cosmopolitans for a relatively modest sum.

One may justifiably protest that the omnipresence of English could lead to the adulteration of other languages, not so much by borrowings that they make from English—this is a normal and universal linguistic phenomenon—as by the distortions in syntax and vocabulary that Anglicisms may impose. In France, Etiemble listed an inventory of such contaminations of the French language in his famous *Parlez-vous franglais?* If abusive or superfluous "Americanisms" do have a tendency to invade other languages, it should nevertheless be stressed that the decay of some "high culture" languages has mostly autonomous causes. There are two principal ones: the decline in educational levels in nations where they were previously high, and a spurious modernism that regards any concern to protect and develop the specific virtues of a language as backward-looking, academic purism. The majority of semantic confusions, improprieties and syntactical inconsistencies that pepper, for example, the French media language are of purely domestic origin. They owe nothing to contamination by English. On the other hand, it is true that the impoverishment of a language makes it more and more vulnerable to invasion by alien terms and structures—as happens today, in the majority of cases, from a bastardized English. Of course, every language must evolve; but it's a mistake to forget that the evolution can be to either good or ill effect. The bombing of a cathedral is certainly one form of architectural innovation, but does that make it desirable?

It remains a fact that in the domain of languages too, globalization leads to variety, not uniformity. The spread of English facilitates communication and mutual influence between cultures; it is hardly a trivial matter when, thanks to the lingua franca, Japanese, Germans, Filipinos, Italians, Russians, French, Brazilians *et al.* can participate in the same colloquium, exchanging information and ideas. Meanwhile, many more people than in the past speak or understand one or two foreign languages other than English in addition to their native language.

■ ■ ■

THE REAL DANGER—conceivably a mortal one—for European culture is that anti-American and antiglobalist phobias might derail progress. Guy Sorman has shown the scientific and technological retreats this obscurantism has led to in his book *Progress and Its Enemies*. And this is neither a "right-wing" nor a "left-wing" thesis; it is a rational one. It is defended alike by the liberal-democrat Sorman and by the socialist Claude Allègre. The latter wages war against the idea that Europe should abandon nuclear energy, genetic engineering and research using embryonic cells. Should the pressure groups that agitate against progress win the day, he writes, in twenty years the European states will regress "to the level of the underdeveloped countries, in a world that will be dominated by the United States and China."* The anti-American fanatics will then have succeeded in making Europe even more dependent on the United States than it is today.

---

* *L'Express,* 7 February 2002.

6. Being "Simplistic"

WHEN RONALD REAGAN delivered the famous speech in which he called the Soviet Union the "Evil Empire" in 1983, he came in for the usual round of pitying, contemptuous sneers; yet it is not apparent that subsequent progress in Soviet studies gives us grounds to call it the "Benevolent Empire."

At the time, most of the oppressed peoples felt relief as they realized that a Western head of state was finally showing some understanding of their unhappy situation. By now, two years into the new century, it is obvious—especially to citizens of the erstwhile "satellites" of Eastern Europe—that President Reagan's policies precipitated the disintegration of the gangster regime based in Moscow that had dominated such a large part of the world for three-quarters of a century; and it is obvious also that the "détente" policies of Reagan's predecessors had served only to prolong the agony.

Nineteen years later, after his January 2002 State of the Union address, George W. Bush was met by a similar chorus of imprecations for calling Iraq, Iran and North Korea an "axis of evil." The president was pointing to countries known or suspected to have assisted international terrorism, which were clandestinely amassing weapons of mass destruction. The French minister of foreign affairs, Hubert Védrine, deplored this "simplistic" analysis that, he said, "reduces all the world's problems to the war against terrorism." And he repeated the old charge that America's "unilateralism" causes her—how dreadful!—to "base her decisions on her own worldview and on the defense of her own interests." Let's note *en passant* that this is an excellent definition of the "independent" foreign policy espoused by General de Gaulle and followed by his successors.

The State of the Union address is the president's report to the nation on the previous year's events. It stands to reason that it would focus on what most concerns his countrymen, and on this occasion it was, of course, the September 11 catastrophe that loomed largest in their thoughts. The president's speech reflected the fact that September 11 had profoundly changed how the United States and the other democracies viewed the problems of defense and diplomacy. But in acknowledging this reality, Bush was by no means reducing all the world's problems to the war against terrorism. Moreover, even in Europe we've lost count of all the books and articles developing the theme that everything has changed, that we are involved in a "new type of war" that is "just beginning." Yet these authors are not saying that the entirety of international relations can be reduced to the war on terrorism. Like Mr. Bush, they are simply warning that the nations of the world, and above all the democracies, must henceforth not shirk facing up to this new and critical challenge.

And President Bush could not have neglected to give priority to the new situation in his speech, when for five months accusations had multiplied that the American intelligence agencies had failed to read prior warning signs and had missed opportunities to forestall the terrorists. Admittedly, the phrase "axis of evil" and the "crusade" proclaimed in September 2001 are somewhat grandiloquent, but may the statesman who has never been guilty of hyperbole throw the first stone! Here the form is assuredly less important than the content, and careful journalists and commentators should have pointed out that this sort of rhetorical style harks back to the foundations of American culture, and that literal translation may create wrong impressions. Similarly, it might seem ridiculous when French political and cultural spokespeople trot out references to France's *rayonnement*—as they habitually do. Taken literally, the word implies that we French consider France to be the sun of humanity, the stellar orb whose function it is to shine down on and warm the entire planet. But fortunately we may doubt that every orator who lapses into this cliché is fully aware of the image of national vanity he is presenting to foreign audiences.

If the response to new threats was not to be unilateral—that is, one-sided—there had to be another side that did more than mutter reproachful litanies, but proposed and implemented concrete strategic policies.

As time passed, it became apparent that Europeans increasingly regarded the 9/11 attacks as an anomalous, distracting interlude. Instead of taking steps to ward off deadly dangers, once again Europeans were showing their propensity for denial.

What a mistake! A new kind of terrorism, directed by highly organized groups, and certainly (or in all likelihood) harbored and assisted by state powers, has been growing relentlessly since the early 1980s. With or without bin Laden, these groups have continued to be active since September 11; several high-level alerts have been issued by the American intelligence agencies since that day. One of them warned of another possible attack on United States territory on February 12, just after President Bush's State of the Union address; the suspects were Yemeni and Saudi Arabian. Evidently the U.S. agencies, having learned their lesson, were striving to keep better tabs on the international terrorist networks. If Europe tends not to perceive the threat to the same degree, perhaps it is because its capacity for military intervention has been considerably reduced over the last ten years, while that of the United States has only increased, widening a strategic gap that may henceforth be impossible to close. Europe has made a principle of powerlessness.

The theory that terrorism derives solely from economic inequalities among nations does not bear scrutiny. Most of the terrorists came from the most comfortable social milieus in the wealthiest Muslim lands; some had gone to Western universities. So the origin of the new hyperterrorism lies in ideology: in the strange world of Islamic extremism.

As Francis Fukuyama writes, "The conflict is not one of clashing civilizations in the sense of equally important cultural zones; it is symptomatic, rather, of a rearguard action fought by people who feel themselves threatened by modernization and by its moral component: respect for human rights." For the jihadists, the ultimate enemy is "the secular character of the Western conception of rights, a conception that lies at the heart of the liberal tradition."* And it is this same liberal tradition, we should note, that is the bête noire of the Western adversaries of globalization.

No one is suggesting that we shouldn't do everything feasible to promote the development of the poorer countries of the world. But aid will

---

*Le Figaro, 26 November 2001.

not suffice if it is diverted or embezzled. The cure must lie in fundamental reforms: good economic management, political democratization, secular education, active measures against corruption, gender equality, freedom of information, religious pluralism and tolerance—in short, everything that Islamic radicalism fiercely hates and struggles against. The path to equality is through modernization: this truth is precisely what the Islamists most despise, for to modernize effectively means deviating from the *sharia*. To those who point out that Christianity adapted to modern civilization and that Islam cannot perpetuate intact a thousand-year-old model of society, they reply that God's instructions, dictated to the Prophet by the archangel Gabriel, are unalterable.* The Islamists seek to modernize without Westernizing. But there are few methods for achieving economic, political and cultural progress aside from those followed by the West for the last few centuries. The Islamists are therefore locked in an irresolvable contradiction, the source of their resentment against the West and above all against the United States. And terrorism is not helping them to escape this contradiction, either. It is not by detonating bombs in the Paris Saint-Michel metro station (as was done in 1995) or by taking the Paris-Miami flight with explosives packed into one's shoes (as an Anglo-Arab terrorist did in December 2001) that one promotes economic growth in developing countries.

To argue that the only way to combat terrorism is by eliminating economic inequalities between nations is not merely to misjudge the reasons for terrorism; it is above all to evade offering practical resistance to it. This eschatological argument, making defense policy contingent on the advent of a perfect universe, grants permission to placidly await the end of the world. For Europeans, this is but a cover for their incapacity to formulate an operational strategy for the here and now. For Americans of the far Left, it is a new avatar of their old "blame America first" posture. With similar sophistry, the pacifists and neutralists during the Cold War preached that the democracies had no right to contain or even criticize totalitarian regimes until they had erased all injustices at home and those within their sphere of influence. In both cases, this indirect way of justifying inaction derives from an identical *idée fixe:* anti-Americanism. And in both cases, this means that right-thinking democ-

---

*See, among others, the distinguished scholar Bernard Lewis's *What Went Wrong: Western Impact and Middle Eastern Response* (Oxford University Press, 2002).

racies ought to dissociate themselves from the American-led coalition and from the alliance to which they owe their security and their liberty.

The European "allies" approve of fighting terrorism in principle, but disapprove of how the United States goes about it. In like manner, during the Cold War they adhered to the Atlantic alliance in principle, while often criticizing—indeed, sometimes opposing—American initiatives, although these were dictated by the key policies of containment and deterrence. One has only to recall the huge demonstrations that inundated Germany, Italy, Greece, France and Spain against the deployment of Pershing missiles in Western Europe, although this was necessary to counterbalance the SS-20 missiles that the Soviet Union had installed in Eastern Europe. If President Mitterrand, invited to speak before the deputies of the Bundestag at the beginning of 1983, courageously argued in favor of these *euromissiles,* the socialists of the German SPD on the other hand remained ferociously hostile. And in that same year, indignant shouts resounded against the American intervention in Grenada, even though it was known that the U.S.S.R. had secretly constructed a military airfield and a submarine base on the island. After Grenada's president was assassinated, thanks to the skill of Cuban agents, the government fell entirely under Soviet control. There were more Cubans on the island than Grenadans. The danger became so evident that the Organization of Eastern Caribbean States requested American intervention. Nothing in this body of commonly acknowledged facts could dissuade the majority in the European media from believing that what they had witnessed was a case of American aggression pure and simple, with no other motivation than Yankee imperialism. I remember when, as a participant at a press lunch in Madrid, I was peppered with questions about the affair. I scandalized many of the Spanish journalists by replying that I viewed the Soviet-Cubans, the agents of the coup d'état, as the real aggressors.

When Ronald Reagan in 1987, at the Berlin Wall, challenged: "Mr. Gorbachev, tear down this wall," shock and scorn poured from the European chancelleries, even in West Germany—except from Helmut Kohl. Clearly, the pathetic Reagan was a public menace. We knew him to be an idiot—and Kohl as well—and we were finding him to be more and more irresponsible every day. Two years later, the Berlin Wall came down under the blows of people who had been oppressed by the Communists, while certain highly intelligent European leaders tied themselves in knots trying to keep the Communist German Democratic Republic alive and to block German reunification. In 2002, that declaration by the dangerously "imbecilic" Reagan greeted visitors at the entrance to an exhibition on the history of Berlin in that very city, once again the capital of a reunified Germany.

These are only a few examples. A host of others equally suggest that if, during the Cold War, the United States had not displayed a minimum of unilateralism vis-à-vis the perennial European advice-givers, the Soviet empire would have endured much longer than it did. The tyrannized peoples know this well; they count Ronald Reagan as one of their great benefactors. Adam Michnik, Poland's most influential editorialist and press magnate, recalls that the Strategic Defense Initiative—the "Star Wars" so decried by Western leftists—was the decisive factor in persuading the Soviets that they could never win the Cold War, for it made patently obvious their irremediable technological inferiority. The SDI was a key trigger of perestroika and the cascade of events that followed.

By contrast with American leaders, Europeans shine more brilliantly in the theatre of ideas (at least in their own estimation) than in the practical realm. But like Reagan, one may be less than a great intellectual and still be a great man of action.

Assessing the strategic analyses of the various battlefronts between the democratic zones and those of their enemies, I warned in 1987 that the experts were overlooking a very important confrontation, one that was not geographically localized: the terror front.* The terrorist phenomenon was—until September 11—consistently underestimated, although it had already taken on the dimensions of a veritable war.

After the 9/11 catastrophe, numerous commentators and public officials, beginning with President George W. Bush himself, expressed the conviction that this was not simply an act of terrorism, but an act of war, even a type of war that was going to become a permanent feature of the twenty-first century. The enormity of the aggression and the staggering number of victims should be enough to justify this diagnosis. However, this was not the first time that terrorism could have been regarded as a form of warfare.

---

*See my book *Le Terrorisme contre la démocratie* (Hachette, Pluriel series, 1987), Preface.

In civil wars, religious wars, ideological wars, wars against a central power in the name of regional loyalties, there is no shortage of examples past and present of terrorism used as a strategic weapon. It is terrorism because there are no regular armies deployed in the service of a state fighting another state, nor even a guerrilla movement contending with a formal army. It is also war, since it entails coordinated actions by multiple organizations in the service of political ends, or what appear to be such to those who pursue them. During the seventies and eighties the Italian Red Brigades, the German Red Army Faction and Direct Action in France had an aim that Clausewitz would have called a war objective: to replace democratic capitalism with Communism. We know now that these criminal associations were advised, trained and financed directly or indirectly by the East Bloc secret services. In effect, these groups were the hot fronts of the Cold War, confirming that terrorism with strategic goals has a long history.

The attacks on the Twin Towers and the Pentagon seemed extraordinary partly because of the large number of victims, but such numbers were not entirely unprecedented. From 1990 to 2001, the Groupe Islamique Armé (GIA) killed between 100,000 and 150,000 people in Algeria, to which must be added those murdered in the Paris attacks of 1995. It's worth recalling that the GIA commando who hijacked an Air France Airbus in 1994 and was overpowered by police at the Marseille-Marignane airport had intended to crash the plane into the Eiffel Tower, killing all the passengers and hundreds of sightseers—a plan prefiguring the Twin Towers operation. These were terrorists, since they used terror to put pressure on the Algerian and French governments (the latter assumed to be the accomplice of the former). Clearly these were people who saw themselves as soldiers prosecuting a war, since they based their activities on a geostrategic analysis and pursued global political objectives. The Italian anarchist who assassinated King Umberto I in 1900 was a terrorist pure and simple, but his crime resulted in no real political change. On the other hand, the assassins who killed the prefect Érignac in Ajaccio in 1998 saw themselves as combatants in an imaginary war between Corsica and France. Their political goal was, first, to free Corsica from the French "yoke" and, second, to pressure the French government into concessions they hoped would lead to the island's autonomy. In the latter they have made some headway.

When U.S. warplanes in 1986 bombed Libya in reprisal for terrorist acts committed in Germany against American military personnel, the
Americans recognized the logic of warfare and acted accordingly. What's
more, Muammar al-Qaddafi did likewise when he launched missiles
against a U.S. Coast Guard station on the Italian island of Lampedusa.
The perennially pious European hypocrites averted their gaze from yet
another perilous cavalry charge by the "B-movie cowboy" who occupied
the White House. The European governments—with the exception of
the British—went so far as to refuse permission for their American "ally's"
aircraft to fly over their territories. By so doing, they were acting as de
facto allies of Qaddafi. This was notably true of France, always the most
eager to prostrate herself before a dictator. For this she was rewarded,
since in 1989, on the orders of Qaddafi, terrorists detonated a bomb
aboard a DC-10 of the French airline UTA, on a Brazzaville-Paris flight,
killing 170 people. Then in 1998 came the destruction of Pan Am flight
103 over Lockerbie, Scotland, with 270 deaths. In Qaddafi's mind, terrorism was war.

Despite all these precedents, the perception that a new epoch began
after September 11, as acknowledged alike by governments, commentators and public opinion generally, was and remains justified. A mutation—a qualitative leap, as philosophers would say—has unquestionably
taken place, transforming the kind of threat that the democracies must
face up to. This is for several reasons: The first is the number of victims,
several thousand exterminated in less than an hour. Such an operation
resembles a military strike more than an act of terrorism, which can kill
as many people but typically over a longer period of time. This is why
people began to speak of "hyperterrorism," defined as a new kind of warfare. A stateless aggressor may act with the same preparatory coordina-
tion and efficiency as a state power. The long strategic planning, the
sophisticated use of international financing, the placement of moles, or
sleepers, in practically every country, the mastery of chemical, biological and even nuclear weaponry—all these add up to a novel phenomenon:
modern terrorism. Modern at least in its means, for it is archaic in its
motivations.

After September 11, there was much talk of a culture clash. But as
Chancellor Gerhard Schroeder aptly put it, in the same vein as Francis
Fukuyama, "It is not a battle between civilizations, it is a battle *for* civi-
lization"—for democratic, secular, multidenominational civilization,

where law is radically separated from religion, where women are legally equal to men, and where freedom of thought allows science and philosophy to flourish. It is this civilization that radical Islam is bent on destroying.

All the theories that explain bin Laden and al-Qaʿida ("the base" in Arabic) as foes of economic inequalities in the world are not pertinent in the least. None of the texts emanating from al-Qaʿida mention such a grievance, any more than they invoke a real or supposed "unilateralism" in American foreign policy, the charge so often leveled against the United States but never by the terrorists, who disdain such trifling preoccupations. The radicals reproach Western civilization for contravening the teachings of the Qur'an in its very existence. By hammering in this notion, they foment the fanaticism that creates suicide bombers.

Let's not deceive ourselves: Islamic hyperterrorism aims to strike at the entire West, not only the United States—although the latter, as the foremost democratic power, is obviously its primary target. In 2000, the New Zealand police arrested an Islamist commando in Auckland who was preparing to bomb a nuclear reactor in Sydney, Australia, during the Olympic Games. Already in 1998, the French antiterrorist unit had foiled jihadists who were planning an attack on the Stade de France in St. Denis during a World Cup soccer game. In November 2001, 360 al-Qaʿida agents were arrested in fifty countries. In Spain, Judge Baltazar Garzon jailed a group of eight suspects on November 18. It is in Europe that the greatest concentration of hyperterrorist cells is to be found. But al-Qaʿida also has not hesitated to attack Muslim countries that have made the mistake of resisting radicalism: for example, Tunisia and Egypt, where there was an assassination attempt against Hosni Mubarak in 1995, and where scores of Western tourists perished as victims of Islamist violence during the 1990s.

■ ■ ■

THUS HYPERTERRORISM BORROWS its technological means from our modern civilization while trying to destroy and replace it globally with an archaic one—an engine of poverty and an enemy of Western values. In these terms the "war of the twenty-first century" is defined.

So it is more and more apparent that the September 11 attacks have transformed our view of international relations. From 1990 to 2000, world diplomacy remained essentially committed to the imperative of wrapping up the Cold War: How could the Communist countries be assisted in their evolution towards democracy and a market economy? How could Central Europe and the Baltic states be brought into NATO and the European Union without provoking Russian anxieties? What was to be done with the old Strategic Arms Limitation Treaties dating from the early 1970s? What policy should be pursued with respect to China, which was in the process of becoming economically capitalist while striving to remain politically totalitarian? How might the Third World be helped towards integration with the developing world economy and make progress in human rights? What evolution was foreseeable in relations between the new American superpower and her allies?

This reading of world affairs, valid for fifty years, was relegated to the past when World War IV—as some commentators don't hesitate to call it—broke out.* The American superpower turned out to be the preferred target of the new hyperterrorism, and it revealed an unexpected vulnerability. Concomitant changes were astoundingly swift and far-reaching. Until the autumn of 2001, Russia's preoccupation had been to defend what remained of its great-power status—if not against the West, then apart from the West. But in 2002, Vladimir Putin no longer raised objections to the entry into NATO of former Warsaw Pact members. Suddenly he stopped protesting against the presence of NATO forces in Kosovo; reversed policy on the subject of the United States' projected abrogation of the ABM treaty, which up till then he had energetically resisted; and agreed to the establishment of American military bases in former Soviet republics of Central Asia. In short, Russia converted itself into a Western power, a metamorphosis that in mid-2001 would have seemed improbable.

Why this turnaround? Because Putin was not slow to grasp the meaning of what had happened. September 11 highlighted how obsolete our ingrained perception of dangers actually was. But for us to realize this fact, the new threats had to impose themselves upon our attention, and on a colossal scale. After the seismic shift, who in Russia can still believe that the chief danger is that the U.S. might fire a missile at Moscow? For what purpose? And in the West, who can possibly maintain that the Moscow of 2002 considers pulverizing Paris, London or New York? These Cold War nightmares are as far from us now as those of the Hundred

---

*Norman Podhoretz, "How to Win World War IV," *Commentary*, February 2002.

Years' War. Dominating today's division are, on one side, the international terrorist groups and "rogue" states, and on the other, the governments that are uniting to protect themselves, including those Muslim countries hostile to the jihadists. In a sense, bin Laden has been a useful instructor in strategy: he has forced us to look in the direction from which tomorrow's threats will come.

For nearly twenty years, terrorist attacks on Western countries—including France (in 1986, 1994 and 1995, in Paris and Algiers, and in 1983 in Libya)—went unpunished. All were considered isolated operations, individual initiatives attributable to fanatics, instead of being analyzed as so many elements in a systematic war. I am referring here to Islamic terrorism, fundamentally distinct from the other terrorisms: Basque, Irish, Corsican, Colombian, Peruvian. From 1983, when Hizbullah, armed by Iran and Syria, killed sixty-three officials at the American embassy in Beirut with a truck bomb; to the attack on the destroyer U.S.S. *Cole* in October 2000, which cost the lives of seventeen sailors; to the first attack on the World Trade Center in 1993, and in the same year the attempted assassination of George Bush père by Saddam Hussein in Kuwait; to the cluster of bombings in 1998 that killed several hundred people in the American embassies at Nairobi and Dar es Salaam: this does not complete the litany of methodical assaults perpetrated by a radical Islam that is ever better organized, commanded, equipped, trained, financed and supplied with fanaticized recruits willing to commit suicidal murder of infidels.

The salient, remarkable fact in these two decades of acts of war, a fact that future historians will point to, is that none of the targeted powers saw fit to take a comprehensive view of the situation or plan the smallest retaliatory measures, except for the United States in 1986 against Qaddafi, to the general consternation of the European democracies. At the time, I found this very surprising. Terrorist cells had been able to flourish in the United States, France, Great Britain, Belgium, Germany and Spain, apparently without causing the police agencies and governments of those nations to suspect their scope and potential. The lesson—which the terrorist networks did not fail to draw—was that the war could be intensified with impunity.

It is in this context that George W. Bush's use of the phrase "axis of evil" must be viewed. Despite cries of alarm from Europeans, it has been proved that the three countries he named had bought, manufactured, sold or given away weapons of mass destruction, arguably enabling terrorists to obtain them. A number of governments, and not only Muslim ones, can be suspected of aiding Islamist terrorists directly or indirectly. In the case of Iran, the mullahs' guilt is common knowledge.

President Bush's choice of words therefore constituted a warning to his countrymen. His message was: Up till now, despite all the attacks against us, we have barely reacted against those countries that we know or suspect to harbor or to have equipped terrorists. Since September 11, everything has changed. From now on, we are at war, and any terrorist attack on American lives or property, at home or abroad, merits a proportional response. As strategic analysts would say, Bush's speech was couched in the vocabulary of "deterrence." A leading Cold War concept, deterrence has regained currency, but in modified form and against another type of threat.

With all due deference to the European critics—to whom Bush no doubt intended to convey a message—it's hard to see what exactly is "simplistic" about this warning. On the contrary, it was altogether well thought out and adapted to the new context of hyperterrorism. It should be added that the three governments indicted by Bush are atrociously repressive regimes, where arbitrary internment and summary execution are the rule—and in the case of Iraq and Korea, even mass extermination. This detail doesn't faze the hyperconscience of the Left in the slightest. For observers of international terrorism, of its strategic bases and state sponsors, there is nothing extreme about assigning these dictatorships to an "axis of evil"; it is a straightforward description. In the eyes of posterity, the passivity, even semicomplicity that certain European governments have shown towards these blood-soaked tyrannies will hardly be reckoned among the most courageous moral stances in our history.

One of the reasons for the superpower's "unilateralism" is that Europeans in general systematically reject American strategic analyses as false, thereby dissociating themselves from the policies that derive from these analyses. This is not always the case, of course; but even when the allies act in concert with America, as they did, for example, in the Gulf War or ten years later in Afghanistan, they rush to wash their hands of any involvement with the practical consequences that logically follow from these operations. Why did they participate in the Gulf War at all, only to take Saddam Hussein's side later when the dictator violated the commitments he had made after his defeat? Thus they wiped out the gains that should have accrued. Why send European troops to Afghanistan in the autumn of 2001, only to deny a year later the continuing existence of a global hyperterrorist threat and downplay the malfeasance of the "rogue" states that support or have the means to support it? As 2002 began, American experts on counterterrorism warned that the strikes against al-Qaʿida had temporarily diminished but not eliminated the threat it posed, and the Bush administration drew up its policies on the basis of this diagnosis. By rejecting that assessment and consequently the policies, Europeans deny themselves participation in the "multilateralism" they are constantly demanding. The argument that the United States could at least take the European objections more into account won't wash, for the objections usually amount to sweeping repudiations of the Americans' entire geostrategic doctrine, condemned as both unsound and dangerous.

The basis for this European attitude is less political than psychological—hence the propensity to twist, willfully forget or invent facts, when the actual facts threaten to undermine an ongoing indictment of the United States. An example: while the European Union was blaming America for preferring confrontation to negotiation with the three countries of the "axis of evil," Iran was refusing to accredit a British ambassador on the grounds that he was "Jewish and an MI6 agent" (the British equivalent to the CIA). But if there are spies in every embassy, the ambassador himself is rarely one of them. Furthermore, the diplomat in question was not Jewish; and were he Jewish, the ayatollahs' pretext would have been no less despicable. The Islamic Republic was not unaware that its allegations were ludicrous; it was simply manifesting its hostility towards the West and spurning two years of efforts by Britain's Foreign Office to improve relations with Tehran. A fine example of "negotiation," the approach so extolled by the European Union! But the E.U. scarcely learned a thing from the contemptuous snub. To do so, it would have had to admit that the United States was at least partially in the right, a concession that would have caused unbearable psychological stress. Yet Washington has clearly stated that it foresees no military operations against Iran, noting that a strong antifundamentalist party and a turbulent current of public opinion—notably among the young—oppose the regime, and that a revolution in favor of democracy is quite possible and deserves to be encouraged.

With regard to North Korea, European inaccuracy verges on outright—even dishonorable—lies. After Bush's speech about the "axis of

evil," a chorus of political and media voices swelled: in leveling his brutal warning against North Korea, lamented these apologists, the U.S.
president was perilously disrupting the rapprochement process between
the two Koreas. But this process had been broken much earlier—six
months before Bush was elected to the White House. Immediately after
the historic visit to Pyongyang by South Korean president Kim Dae Jung,
the North Korean dictator, Kim Jong Il, undertook to sabotage the "Sun-
shine Policy" that was meant to foster détente. The North, preoccupied
above all with preserving totalitarianism, in practice managed to neutralize the South's well-meaning efforts, contenting itself with extorting
money while conceding nothing in exchange. The United States had
promoted a "warming" of relations between the two countries for six
years and had lavished substantial aid on the North—while the Europeans continued to support the Pyongyang totalitarianism with the gulli-
bility that comes naturally to them when they deal with tyrannies.

The capital of North Korea has for years been one of the favorite
destinations for political tourism. In 1994 the United States negotiated
an agreement with Pyongyang whereby the Americans would supply the
North Korean government aid in the form of food, oil and the means to
build two nuclear power plants for civil energy production. In exchange,
Pyongyang agreed to suspend its strategic nuclear program and missile
sales to other countries. Naturally, Kim Jong Il pocketed the aid pay-
ments and pushed ahead with his weapons programs anyway, evading
effective inspections.

In 1998 the dictator sent a ballistic missile soaring over Japan as a
reminder of his capabilities. It is estimated that since 1985, North Korea
has sold at least 540 missiles to Libya, Iran and other entirely trustwor-
thy countries. Since 1998, it has sold 480 Scud missiles to Iraq, Iran and
Egypt. When the Little Stalin of Pyongyang is requested to cease his arms
racket, he replies that he can't possibly do without the cash it brings in.
Yet when bribe money to refrain is showered on him, he continues
unabashed.

The political pilgrims carry on their missions to Pyongyang, convinced that they are engaging in high diplomacy as they offer credits in
exchange for rebuffs and broken promises. In June 2000 it was the president of South Korea, Kim Dae Jung, who went begging for the honor
of footing the bills. In the autumn of 2000, Madeleine Albright, U.S. secretary of state, attended the festivities celebrating the fiftieth anniversary

of the North Korean Communist Party, her mission being to prepare for an official visit by President Clinton—which, in the event, did not transpire. Then came the turn of a Belgian parliamentary delegation, which in spring 2001 was "over the top in obsequiousness"—I quote *Le Monde*—and was widely ridiculed. In May a delegation from the E.U., led by the prime minister of Sweden, came to pay homage; some countries (but fortunately not France) promised to establish diplomatic relations with Pyongyang, without receiving anything in return.

Nevertheless, apart from its Soviet-supplied nuclear and missile technologies, North Korea is one of the weakest nations in the world. It is economically moribund, devastated by the collectivist scourge. Experts estimate that from one to two million people have died of starvation since 1990, out of a population of twenty-two million. Flocks of orphaned children search amid the refuse for scraps of food. In one decade, life expectancy declined by six years. And this while the country was receiving generous aid: by May of 2001, Washington had delivered 100,000 metric tons of food and the E.U. had spent 200 million euros on relief. But again we see what little likelihood there is of aid actually getting to populations in need. There is every reason to think that these donations have served instead to boost the regime's military arsenal: in 1994, at the height of the famine, North Korea purchased forty submarines from Russia.

Of the Communist remnants that linger on, North Korea is the cruelest and most criminal. It is a totalitarian barracks of pitiless repression, of crowded concentration camps and frequent public executions. Polite appeals to human rights by smiling visitors from democratic nations are dismissed by Kim Jong Il and his junta with unwavering contempt. In the humanitarian as in the strategic domain, the humble prayers of the political pilgrims are never answered, even when accompanied by substantial offerings.

The pilgrims' aims are clearly praiseworthy: to open North Korea to democracy, turn its economy around and, in the long run, reunite it with South Korea. Unfortunately, these goals cannot be achieved without first satisfying a condition that Kim Jong Il and his nomenklatura will never agree to: removal of their regime. But the diplomacy of pilgrimage and unilateral concessions serves only to shore up tyranny and postpone its long-overdue demise.

Despite his criticisms of North Korea, George W. Bush renewed his offers to negotiate, but to no avail. He even kept financial aid going for oil deliveries and construction of the two nuclear power plants. And he continued to grant North Korea generous humanitarian relief, principally in the form of food supplies, as did South Korea, Japan, China and Europe. But Kim Jong Il neither returned to the negotiating table, nor did he accede to the agreed-upon inspections and controls of his weapons of mass destruction. These are the facts, difficult for those of good faith to forget and easy enough to verify. "In exchange for hundreds of millions of dollars in humanitarian aid," said the *New York Times* on May 4, 2001, "in exchange for all the investments made by South Korean companies, most of which lost money, North Korea has done practically nothing to dismantle its preparations for war in the peninsula."

In view of such stubbornness, one may concede that the United States is not being altogether irrational in exerting pressure on this dangerous government. This is even truer in the case of Iraq, the only country in the "axis of evil"—at least so far—against which the Bush administration has envisaged direct military action. Europeans are free to dissociate themselves from the United States' posture towards the three countries concerned, but they have no proposals of their own for dealing with terrorism and the proliferation of weapons of mass destruction. To keep on repeating, as they always do, that a "political solution" must be found is to blow hot air: Saddam Hussein has rejected every diplomatic avenue proposed to him since 1990. By persisting in using such an empty phrase when confronted by this thug, Europeans are betraying their unwillingness to face up to what could be their most urgent national security problem. Forfeiting the game, they have no standing to fume against the Americans' unilateralism; it is a unilateralism of the Europeans' own making.

After Bush's 2002 State of the Union address, Hubert Védrine, the French minister of foreign affairs, clarified that his remark about American *simplisme* entailed not the slightest "aggressiveness" on his part. This is pure Védrine. His constant attacks on the United States, if we are to believe him, are merely expressions of goodwill. He animadverted, "There is perhaps more anti-French feeling in the U.S. than there is anti-Americanism in France."

I happen to disagree. Of course, given that putting down the U.S. is the favorite pastime of the French intelligentsia, the patience of Americans is tested to the limit and they frequently fire back broadsides of their own, especially in the press. But outside these polemical exchanges, I have never noticed in America the same kind of fundamental ill will towards France or the French that one witnesses in France towards the Americans.

Seldom has this malevolence been more obvious than in the affair of the al-Qaᶜida terrorists held at Guantanamo. Among the organizations set up to defend "human rights," there are some that seem only to do so when it is a matter of exonerating the worst enemies of the democracies and preventing democracies from protecting themselves. These virtuous leagues have often joined forces to protest the imprisonment of ETA assassins far from the Basque Country, a removal obviously intended to make it more difficult for them to keep in contact with accomplices who were still at liberty. And when bin Laden's henchmen were interned at Guantanamo, the same curious human rights organizations became even more zealous, demanding that the detainees be granted the status of prisoners of war as defined by the Geneva Convention. Yet however much one looks at the Convention, giving the widest possible latitude to its definitions, one cannot see how a combatant in the uniform of a regular army and taken prisoner can be compared to a terrorist in civilian clothes passing unnoticed among the populace in time of peace, killing randomly and without warning in a city street, an airplane, an embassy, a church. Do those who cut the throat of journalist Daniel Pearl and then decapitated him, who made a point of recording the scene and sending the cassette to his widow, deserve to be treated as prisoners of war? "Daniel Pearl was an American," writes Denis Jeambar, editor of *L'Express*, "but first he was a journalist, and as such he was a defender of the universal values of freedom of thought and freedom of the press.... Those indignant French and European voices, so quick to denounce the treatment of the Taliban prisoners at Guantanamo, therefore ought to have rung out loud and clear. But we heard nothing, alas. Or very little."[*]

The al-Qaᶜida supporters have been held at Guantanamo to preclude escape and, through interrogation, to obtain information about planned operations—so as to forestall more events like the attack on the Twin Towers. Are the so-called defenders of the Rights of Man anxious, then, to see further murders carried out?

So it seems. For they also railed, both in Europe and in the United States, against the modest antiterrorist security measures that the authorities put into force in the democracies after September 11. We heard shouts

---

[*] *L'Express*, 28 February 2002.

that these measures, intended to make it easier for the police to inter-
cept arms or explosives, would destroy our liberties and abolish our constitutional rights. But as Hervé Algalarrondo rightly observes, "Exactly
how, for example, does allowing police to search cars, under certain well-
defined conditions, prejudice our liberties? Customs officers have always
been able to do it, and this hasn't bothered anyone."* The author points
out that Robert Badinter, the celebrated former minister of justice and
former president of the Constitutional Council, a man no one suspects
of harboring hostility to liberty, has upheld the legitimacy of the measures in question by arguing: "The rule of law is not the rule of weakness." No one, remarks Algalarrondo, has taken the trouble to reply to
Badinter.

And for a very good reason: at the root of this upside-down crusade
for liberty lies a hatred for liberty and for democracy, a hatred only intensified when democracy goes under the name of the United States. Here
we encounter the "intellectuals" who thought that in the September 11
attacks, the Americans were only getting a taste of "what they deserved,"
or even that the attacks had never really happened as claimed. (Crazy as
it is, the latter thesis had a brief run in France and was eagerly propa-
gated by the French media.) So the terrorist metro bombers and their
like are really freedom fighters, authentic heroes who unfortunately are
too often repulsed by the Americanized global enemies of freedom. "The
very idea of liberty is fading from people's consciousness," writes the
French philosopher Jean Baudrillard. "... Liberal globalization is going
in exactly the opposite direction: towards a global police state, total control and the reign of a security terrorism."**

Reading this, who would dare argue that France can no longer boast
a great thinker?

■ ■ ■

Even when critiques of the United States are justified, these critiques are
liable to contradict each other and are frequently inconsistent with what
we Europeans profess and practice. Take, for example, the March 2002
decision by the Bush administration to levy a 30 percent tax on imported

---

*Sécurité: la gauche contre le people, (Robert Laffont, 2002).
**Le Monde, 3 November 2001.

steel. This was supposed to protect a declining steel industry in which bankruptcies were multiplying; but it was really an opportunistic political decision taken under pressure by shareholders, workers' unions and lobbyists. From the larger economic point of view, it was an awful course to take and was immediately denounced as such in the United States, with Republicans in the forefront. George F. Will, the prominent conservative commentator, accused George W. Bush of having "cooked up an unpalatable confection of tariffs and import quotas that mock his free trade rhetoric."

The European and Asian protests were not only justified but largely echoed in political and journalistic circles in the U.S., especially because this protectionist policy would raise the price of steel in the American domestic market. But Europeans, and antiglobalists generally, ever ready to lambaste the *libéralisme sauvage* they attribute to America, are poorly positioned to stand in judgment over this or other instances of American protectionism. We would like to know which is the most harmful: free trade or tariff barriers?

European intellectual incoherence is amplified by a contradiction between their principles and their actions. The French are champions at this game of double-dealing. This could be seen a few days after Bush's decision on the steel issue, when the fifteen E.U. members gathered in Barcelona on March 16 to discuss the liberalization of the European energy market. Debate on this question had been dragging on for years; it had been on the agendas of previous summit meetings at Lisbon and Stockholm, without any progress being made. Nor did it go anywhere in Barcelona, for a reason that focused the attention of the press: France's obstructive tactics. In violation of agreed-upon commitments and even signed treaties, specifically Article 86 of the Treaty of Rome, which provided for free market competition, French obstinacy once again postponed its implementation in the energy domain. President of the Republic Jacques Chirac and Prime Minister Lionel Jospin, bitter rivals in the electoral campaign then in progress, temporarily joined forces in order to wage their patriotic battle against liberty.

Why? Because they feared the social troubles that would inevitably ensue if they even began to consider privatizing one of the most ferocious public sector dinosaurs: the state power company, Électricité de France (EDF), which is in the hands of the Communist-controlled labor-union federation, the CGT (Confédération Générale du Travail). A monopoly of a monopoly, the latter's omnipotence is challenged only by an even more extreme antiliberal syndicate: Sud. Like other public sector jugger-nauts, the EDF has at its disposal formidable means of retaliation that governments rarely have the courage to challenge, especially during an election; hence the glorious French stand against the E.U. in Barcelona.

A competitive market would significantly lower the price of gas and electricity for French consumers, and consequently increase household purchasing power and lower the price of consumer goods. Once more, as is usual in France, a powerful organized lobby succeeded in maintain-ing its dominant position and benefits at the expense of the consumer and taxpayer. Lionel Jospin's assertion in Barcelona that the cost of elec-tricity in Europe is lower than in the United States runs counter to the well-known fact that it is 30 percent higher; and in those European coun-tries where energy production has been liberalized—Scandinavian coun-tries, Great Britain and Germany—prices have dropped by nearly 25 percent. Mme Loyola de Palacio, European commissioner for energy, estimates that an excessively state-controlled energy market costs the member nations 15 billion euros every year.* Yet France has extracted a concession from the other countries of the E.U. to delay the opening up of her domestic energy market until 2003, and not until 2004 for pri-vate enterprises and 2005 for the ordinary consumer. Assuming that by these dates France has not extorted yet another postponement—promises made in Lisbon were not kept in Stockholm, and promises made in Stock-holm were not kept in Barcelona—we can meanwhile be astonished at this decision to inflict on millions of people the penalty of having to pay more than they should for their gas and electricity, and for a year longer than businesses will have to. And this is the welfare state of Europe!

It's true that everything was irrational in Barcelona, since on top of it all, three hundred thousand antiglobalizers sacked the city to show their dislike of free trade, just after the European nations at France's insti-gation had spontaneously fulfilled their wishes. With comparable logic, already described in Chapter 2, the antiglobalizers had done their worst in Seattle three years earlier when they opposed the World Trade Orga-nization while demanding trade regulation, although the WTO has exactly that function: the regulation of international trade! It has, for example, repeatedly condemned the United States (again in January 2002)

---

*Interview with *Figaro Économie,* 15 March 2002.

for having allowed American companies to relocate their export profits to tax havens, a form of indirect subsidy.*

The enormous, chronic U.S. trade deficit, while inconvenient for Americans, is an advantage for the rest of the world. When the American economy slows down, as it did in 2001, the global economy also takes a downturn as orders from the world's greatest market decline. In 2000, dozens of countries, from Thailand to Nigeria, sent more than 10 percent of their gross national product to the United States, which buys 6 percent of the goods and services produced by the entire world, in which, therefore, six workers out of a hundred depend on American clients.*

It is in the interests of Europe and Asia, Latin America and Africa, just as much if not more than the United States, to maintain the conditions for unrestricted trade. This fact explains the cries of dismay when the Americans make the slightest protectionist gesture, and clearly demonstrates that the reactionary chants against free trade are absurd.

---

*The details of this WTO condemnation of the United States can be found in an article by Laurence Tovi in the 15 January 2002 issue of *Les Échos.*

7. Scapegoating

THERE IS A BIG DIFFERENCE between being anti-American and being critical of the United States. Once again: critiques are appropriate and necessary, provided that they rest on facts and address real abuses, real errors and real excesses—without deliberately losing sight of America's wise decisions, beneficent interventions and salutary policies. But critiques of this kind—balanced, fair and well-founded—are hard to find, except in America herself: in the daily press, in weekly news magazines, on television and radio, and in highbrow monthly journals, which are more widely read than their equivalents in Europe.

Anti-Americanism is at base a totalizing, if not a totalitarian, vision. The peculiar blindness of fanaticism can be recognized in the way it seizes on a certain behavior of the hated object and sweepingly condemns it, only to condemn with equal fervor the opposite behavior shortly after—or even simultaneously. We have already looked at a good many examples of this type of contradiction, and in this chapter I shall point out some others. According to this vision—in the sense that Littré confers on the word: a "phantom projection, a credulous fantasy of fears, dreams, delusions, superstitions"—Americans can do nothing but speak idiocies, make blunders and commit crimes; and they are answerable for all the setbacks, all the injustices and all the sufferings of the rest of humanity.

Anti-Americanism thus defined is less a popular prejudice than a parti pris of the political, cultural and religious elites. Some would argue that the Muslim "street" we hear so much about, the street that chants "Death to America," represents the masses; but since almost no Muslim country is democratic, it is difficult to assess whether protests of this type are spontaneous or state-organized. In countries whose governments have declared war on the fundamentalists, it is the imams, with their inflammatory and xenophobic sermons, who stir up the emotions of the crowds. The latter, for the most part, are illiterate and unable to access independent sources of information; and in any case censorship prevails, above all on radio and television.

In Iran, since at least 1995, the ayatollahs of the Islamic Republic can no longer conceal the fact that the populace, especially those between ages 15 and 25, no longer follows them in their demonizing of the Great Satan and openly shows a liking for American products, entertainments and lifestyles. This predilection is not the result of American "cultural imperialism," as tearful Europeans are always accusing. The theocratic, obscurantist and sanguinary tyranny of the ayatollahs oppresses and impoverishes the Iranian people while dictating morality by inquisitorial and brutal methods. Allah's police cruelly persecute young people, who are more anxious than their parents to embrace modern life. In this suffocating environment, American civilization, even in its most trivial aspects, appears to the Iranians to be the bringer not of imperialism but of liberty—as it has appeared so often before to so many people in so many parts of the world.

Nothing prevented Europe from playing the role of freedom-bringer in the Middle East; if it didn't do so, it was because once again, through pure anti-Americanism, it saw fit to recommend "dialogue": that is, complicity with tyrants and not with their victims. If Iranians one day achieve democracy, they will owe little to the Europeans, any more than will the Iraqis when they are finally delivered from their cruel despot.

The same contrast can be seen in China: official anti-Americanism on the one hand and a popular appetite for everything American on the other. "To compare how we lived ten years ago with how we live today is like comparing Earth with Heaven," said one Chinese to an American journalist. "The Americans are not just selling us their products—they're selling us a culture," he added, "and it's a culture that lots of Chinese want. They're saying: when you buy an American product, you're buying into a new way of life."* Perhaps a deceptive impression, but not without basis in historical reality.

---

*Elizabeth Rosenthal, "In China, a Big Appetite for Americana," *International Herald Tribune,* 26 February 2002.

In Latin America, emotional currents are ruled by a very old grudge: the grudge of an America that failed against an America that succeeded, a trauma analyzed in Carlos Rangel's superb book, *The Latin Americans: Their Love-Hate Relationship with the United States.** Here again it is the political leadership and above all the intellectuals who perpetuate the resentment, at the price of a profoundly split personality, since most of them are disciples and clients of the United States even as they vituperate the U.S. when they harangue their citizens. The people more or less echo these resentments, even though the disparity between North and South America has been considerably reduced since 1950—which doesn't prevent some country or other from sliding back into the aberrations of the past. But popular anti-Americanism is more conformist than militant and is accompanied by the omnipresent desire to have some share in the North American economy and culture.

It is in Europe that the gap between elites and ordinary citizens is easiest to gauge, thanks to sophisticated polling techniques. According to a SOFRES** survey of May 2000, only 10 percent of French people feel dislike for the United States. Commenting on this poll, historian Michel Winock concludes that "anti-Americanism is not an attitude of the average French person; it is typical of a certain segment of the elites." He notes that one of its causes in the twentieth century was the influence of Communism on huge sectors of the French intelligentsia, but he recalls also that since the nineteenth century, animosity and scorn towards the U.S. came from the intellectual Right, which since then has scarcely reconsidered its harsh judgment. Winock points out that in the time of the Bourbon Restoration (1814–1830), the Vicomte de Bonald saw in America only conformism, materialism, bourgeois values, lack of culture and idolizing of money.

Another historian, Laurent Theis, summarizing "two hundred years of thwarted love" between the two peoples, relates that during the nineteenth century the old affection felt by the French for the Americans since the time of Lafayette was replaced by an aversion, already pushed to fever pitch. Theis writes: "Then appear the name and the image of the Northern Yankee at the antipodes of the noble Southern planter.

---

*Harcourt, 1997.
** *Société française d'enquêtes par sondage,* French public opinion poll institute. See the 25–26 November 2001 issues of *Le Monde.*

Brutish instincts, carnal appetites and pecuniary passions" and, naturally, Bible-thumping hypocrisy—these stereotypes, spouted by publicists of every stripe, stood previously received ideas on their head.* American democracy, revealing itself to be a brute world of the "survival of the fittest," no longer inspired dreams. The noble savage, the pure and valiant young woman, the austere Quaker became comedic figures. What was "this nation of ignorant shopkeepers and narrow-minded industrialists, which, throughout a vast continent, cannot boast one single work of art?" asked Stendhal. What could one say about a country that was "without a single opera house"?

This was typical of what emanated from the tiny slice of French society who were pen-pushers by calling and could vent their opinions in public forums. What did those other French, the French who were not writers of one sort or another, think of America, if they thought about it at all? This is very hard to say. In our time, though, we have a fairly good idea. After September 11, according to another opinion poll, 52 percent of French people interviewed said they had always felt warmly towards the United States and another 9 percent said that their opinion had recently changed in the United States' favor (against 32 percent and 1 percent who said the opposite).**

Nineteenth-century European intellectuals believed that America was a cultural void; but the real void was located in their own inadequate knowledge. It was not until 1856, when Charles Baudelaire translated Edgar Allan Poe, that Europeans began to realize there might be something that could be called literature in the United States. But the myth of cultural barbarism, of a people enslaved by their own addiction to money (an addiction obviously quite unknown to the more idealistic Europeans) lasted until the mid-twentieth century, when it was refuted by reality. Then the greatest outpouring of patronage ever seen went into building and maintaining thousands of museums and universities—and even the opera houses whose absence Stendhal had deplored.

Suddenly the sneers changed to remonstrations: the cultural vacuity of America was transformed overnight into "cultural imperialism." The empty cup was found to be flooding over. In this domain as in everything

---

*Le Point, 28 September 2001.
**SOFRES, May 2000; Le Monde, 25–26 November 2001.

else, the Americans can never be in the right, no matter what they do. Clearly it was a great mistake for Congress in 2002 to pass the highest budget ever for research funding: over $100 billion (to which must be added private investments, as generous as anywhere else in the world). Conversely, expenditures on research in France continued to decline—which didn't prevent the French medical-political complex from brandishing aloft the flag of cultural superiority.*

Despite her alleged indifference towards the life of the mind, it was in America that the first mandatory, free elementary education was introduced, in New York in 1832—fifty years before Jules Ferry instituted similar policies in France—and then soon after in the other states. The precocious literacy that resulted partly explains the early and rapid economic take-off of the United States, which is another cause of anti-American bitterness. In *The Infancy of the World*, Emmanuel Todd shows how decisive this factor is.** Any country that succeeds in "taking off" must cross a critical threshold of literacy: 50 percent of the population, or more significantly 70 percent of those between 15 and 25 years of age. Thus Sweden and Switzerland, countries that by the mid-nineteenth century were still almost entirely rural, were nevertheless the most literate in Europe, which was one of the keys to their rapid industrial development subsequently. By contrast, in 1848 at least 50 percent of the French population were illiterate, and a substantial part of those did not speak French.

American advances in democratizing education did not, of course, register in the mind of the Vicomte de Bonald, a condescending monarchist who rejected any form of democracy and thus could not grasp that democratic government, economic liberalism and public education could be linked to prosperity in any way. Nor did he understand—and in this he was far from alone in Europe before Tocqueville and even after the publication of Tocqueville's great work—the advance that the United States made in establishing universal suffrage for men in 1820.† For women also, America was ahead of the other democracies. Women could vote

---

*See Olivier Postel-Vinay's article in the April 2002 issue of *La Recherche*. France is ranked 14th among the 29 member nations of the OECD (Organization for Economic Cooperation and Development), which consists of the most developed countries in the world (including Greece, Mexico and Poland at the lower end of the scale).

**Seuil, 1984.

†This happened in 1848 in France.

in Wyoming beginning in 1869, followed by eleven other states between 1869 and 1914, and then by the entire nation in 1920. In France, women had to wait until 1944.

These facts are elementary, yet they run up against a European unwillingness to admit that the United States might be a real democracy. If we can easily deny them this honor, even more so do Africans and Latin Americans—whose authority on the topic of democracy is self-evident. We are familiar with the usual themes of anti-American diatribes: slavery, discrimination against blacks, capital punishment, indulgence towards Latin American dictators.

In his book *Tous Américains* ("All Americans Now")* the editor of *Le Monde,* Jean-Marie Colombani, explains why he felt justified in entitling an editorial in his newspaper, the day after 9/11, "We Are All Americans." Hostile reactions to his editorial and the title he had chosen were numerous and immediate, both among readers of *Le Monde* and on the editorial board. This stemmed from the Left's disinclination, even after the massacres in New York and Washington, to renounce its demonized image of the United States, an image that it needs all the more since socialism has ended in shipwreck. If the Good that this cult worshipped has foundered, it consoles itself by continuing at least to execrate the antithetical Evil. Woe upon those who would deprive them of the convenient Lucifer that is their last ideological lifeline.

It takes courage and self-abnegation to argue, as Colombani does, against fanaticism, which has precisely the function of sheltering the mind from any argument. Colombani first recalls that in writing his article in the heat of the moment he was responding to his own feelings of compassion and decency; then he goes on to some political and historical recollections that crush the nutty idea that America has never been a force for the defense and propagation of liberty. He evokes the liberation of Europe in 1944–1945, sarcastically asking if it would have been necessary to send the liberating U.S. Army away so as to "reject America and its racial segregation ... a country that was supporting Ibn Saud and the dictator Somoza in Nicaragua."

Such reservations have some foundation in fact. But if they suffice to establish that America has not always been democratic, then France and Great Britain likewise have not always been democratic. The history

---

*Fayard, 2002.

of Africa and Asia swarms with dictatorships of every type that were supported by the French and the British. Between 1945 and 1965 the United States eliminated all segregation, legally at least, thanks to a voluntary action by the federal government and the Supreme Court against the traditionally racist states. During the same period, France undertook rearguard wars in Indonesia, Madagascar and North Africa, entailing the use of torture and summary executions on a vast scale, with civilian victims numbering in the hundreds of thousands. But it would very much surprise French living under the Fourth Republic and the early Fifth Republic if you told them that they didn't live in a democratic country.

It is likewise in the matter of the death penalty. I count myself among those who would like to see the United States abolish it. Twelve states have done so; that is not enough. But it must be remembered that the federal government does not always have the power to impose its preferences on state legislators, who adopt or repeal laws according to the voters' wishes. And some countries that have only recently abolished capital punishment—the United Kingdom in 1964 and France in 1980—have a tendency towards forgetfulness when they drape themselves in the robes of humanitarianism and accuse the United States of being undemocratic. Should we determine that around 1937, at the time of our own Popular Front, the French Republic was not a democracy because it dexterously plied the guillotine? Acceptance or rejection of barbarous penalties depends more on the evolution of moral attitudes and sensibilities than on the nature of political institutions. As the twenty-first century begins, eighty-seven countries practice capital punishment—some of them, such as China, in massive doses and with no guarantees that the defendant's rights will be respected. But the international anathemas concentrate on the United States, evoking suspicion that they are aimed less at the death penalty itself than at America. How else to explain that what is disgraceful in Austin is pardonable in Beijing or Lhasa?

■ ■ ■

THUS WE ENCOUNTER the two most glaring traits of obsessive anti-Americanism: selectivity with respect to evidence and indictments replete with contradiction.

As an example of the former, take the case of Somoza. Here, we are told, is indisputable proof that Americans back reactionary dictators. But what are we to make of the political and economic campaign waged by the United States against the Dominican dictator Rafael Trujillo? Before he was assassinated in 1961, he had been brought to his knees by the economic sanctions imposed on him by the United States and by the Latin American countries at the behest of the U.S. (within the framework of the Organization of American States). These sanctions against a caudillo of the extreme Right were much more severe than those imposed later on Fidel Castro. And apropos of Castro, not many journalists or politicians mention that he took power with the aid of the CIA. Washington wanted to end Fulgencio Batista's dictatorship and organized his downfall with Castro's help.* And on January 7, 1959, the United States was the second country, after Venezuela, to formally recognize the new Havana regime. It was only later, when Castro established a Stalinist dictatorship on the island and began taking orders from Moscow, that the U.S. turned against him. Here the anti-Americans slyly pick and choose from the evidence, but at least they appeal to facts, however vaguely. Yet America-haters can push virtuosity to the point where they dispense with facts entirely.

The nadir was reached in March 2002 with the publication of *L'Effroyable Imposture* by one Thierry Meyssan. According to Meyssan, no airplane was crashed into the Pentagon on September 11. Rather it was a truck bomb, part of a massive disinformation campaign cooked up by the American secret services and the "military-industrial complex" in order to justify to an appalled nation the upcoming armed interventions in Afghanistan and Iraq. Now, anyone is free to concoct some amusing theory out of whole cloth—for example, that France's defeat in 1940 was a pure invention of the Right so that Marshal Pétain might have an excuse to make a change of political regimes. But snickers would quickly give way to worry if hundreds of thousands of people gave credence to such a crackpot notion. Well, this is what happened in France when we were faced with the lucubrations of Monsieur Meyssan. Not only did radio and television complacently transform themselves into resonance chambers for his drivel, but his book was an immediate and gigantic bestseller. This stampede towards the absurd speaks volumes about French credulity, and it inspires painful perplexity as to the intellectual level of "the most intelligent people on the planet."

---

*See Tad Szulc's *Fidel: A Critical Portrait* (New York: Morrow, 1986).

The second of the above-mentioned symptoms is the frequent recourse to contradictory charges that come one after another only to cancel each other out, and the accusers are seemingly unaware of their incoherence. Fine examples of this tendency can be gleaned from the treatment of Middle Eastern affairs. To be sure, the European commentators' indictments are also full of holes thanks to their selectivity. A single instance: it has become axiomatic by dint of repetition that Israel "invaded" Lebanon in 1982 because Ariel Sharon wanted to go after Arafat in Beirut, and that he is taking revenge today because the PLO chief escaped him. As minister of defense, however, Sharon had no power to decide on war by himself. But there is another little detail that is forgotten: Israel intervened in response to Syria's invasion and four-year-long occupation of Lebanon. The Syrian forces destroyed half of Beirut with their Soviet-made arsenals in 1978, and were approaching closer by the day to Israel's border. I am not an expert in Middle Eastern affairs, but I do take an interest in the workings of the human mind: why is this cause-and-effect sequence of well-known historical events routinely truncated and reduced to its last episode when it is brought up by our pundits in the context of the Israeli-Palestinian crisis of 2000–2002? Because it must be "demonstrated" at any cost that Sharon was bent on "revenge" for his failure to capture Arafat in 1982. I am aware of Sharon's mistakes, but there is no need to ascribe to him others that he did not commit.

Throughout this crisis there was no more instructive spectacle than the swaying waltz of European opinion around United States policies. After having long complained that Americans considered themselves the only competent players in the Middle East, we severely blamed George W. Bush for his passivity and shirking of duty when he stood aloof and made no effort to resolve the crisis. When the United States finally announced that action would be taken, we objected that any such initiative would be so one-sidedly pro-Israel as to deprive it of all legitimacy. But when Bush and his national security advisor, Condoleezza Rice, gave notice to Israel to leave occupied Palestinian territories "without delay," we immediately proclaimed that their demands would be futile and that Secretary of State Colin Powell's projected trip to the area would achieve nothing.

It is not the outright mistakes or the false attributions in these assessments that are most serious; it is their mutual incompatibility. What is striking is our apparent incapacity to acknowledge that we are mistaken when events show that we are.

151

All in all, European governments, media and public opinion think that the United States has consistently and unfairly given its support to Israel. But when the United States adopted a neutral attitude and backed off from direct involvement in the Middle East, Europe indignantly accused Washington of abjuring its responsibilities. And when, at the beginning of April 2002, the president sent several emissaries to Israel and forcefully recommended, in a virtual ultimatum, that Prime Minister Sharon withdraw his troops from the Palestinian Territories "not tomorrow, but at once and without delay," the clarity of this position did little to prompt a realization that the thesis of the United States' unvarying and "unconditional" support of Israel was false. Neither did it induce a rethinking of another (and entirely incompatible) thesis: that of America's egotistical indifference to the Middle Eastern drama. In March and April of 2002, the United States voted with the United Nations Security Council to condemn Israel and to set up a U.N. commission of enquiry on the possible war crimes committed by the Israelis in Jenin; this did nothing to prevent the French radio pundits from continuing to assert, with imperturbable aplomb, that Washington *always* vetoes Security Council motions unfavorable to Israel.

Henry Kissinger says with good reason, "For thirty years, American diplomacy was the catalyst of almost all the progress made by the peace process toward rapprochement between Israelis and Arabs, and especially the Palestinians." A quick recapitulation confirms this. In addition to Kissinger's 1972–1976 shuttle diplomacy between Jerusalem, Cairo, Damascus and Amman, in 1978 President Carter presided over the Camp David meeting between Prime Ministers Sadat and Begin. This summit led to the peace treaty between Egypt and Israel that was signed in Washington in 1979. As for the peace process between the Palestinians and Israel, this was inaugurated at the Madrid conference of 1991. It continued in 1993 with the Oslo Accord, ratified in Washington in December of that year by Yitzhak Rabin and Yasir Arafat, who shook hands in the presence of President Clinton and the cameras of the entire world. This was the American-inspired "Declaration of Principles" concerning Palestinian autonomy. It was followed, again at the urging of the Americans, by the Tabah (in Egypt) Accord, also known as "Oslo II," which deals with "the extension of the Palestinian Authority to the entire West Bank." Then in 1998 came the Wye Plantation (Maryland) Memorandum, followed by the Sharm al-Sheikh Accord, which concerned the implementation of the memorandum. Finally, in July of 2000, President Clinton met at Camp David with Arafat and the Israeli prime minister, Ehud Barak.

A controversy surrounds this last Camp David conference, which required the presence and full attention of the president of the United States for no less than fifteen days. It is supposed that Arafat's "intransigence," which would lead him to reject Barak's "generous proposals" and derail the peace process, was a ploy to make Ariel Sharon's subsequent electoral victory inevitable and hypocritically encourage Palestinian terrorism. Arafat certainly shares some responsibility for the collapse of the peace process. But the story of what really transpired at Camp David seems in reality more complex.* I will make no attempt to clarify this matter here; my intention is not to come up with answers to the Middle Eastern question, but to portray European reactions to the American diplomacy that was grappling with the problem.

These reactions were, at the least, both unjustified and incoherent. Unjustified too was the obsessive and ritual grievance according to which the United States acted "unilaterally" during the crisis—that is, without consulting the Europeans. Secretary of State Colin Powell had in fact preceded his April 2002 Middle Eastern mission with a stopover in Madrid. (Spain was then filling the office of the E.U. presidency.) There he consulted with the foreign affairs ministers of the fifteen E.U. members and with Javier Solana, foreign affairs minister for the Union; nor was Russia excluded from the discussions. Such conduct can hardly be taxed with unilateralism. Kofi Annan, the U.N. secretary-general, underlined by his presence the multilateral character of the negotiations. Yet between them, the European nations were unable to lay a single concrete proposal on the table, not a single realistic plan of action. Not only were they unable to agree with the United States, which goes almost without saying, but they were unable to agree with each other. It is true that the discussion was complicated by the problem of Iraq, which Powell considered inseparable from the Israeli-Palestinian conflict and from the war against terrorism, but which the Europeans didn't fail to shrink timorously away from.

---

*I refer the reader to the long and detailed article by Robert Malley and Hussein Afghan, "Camp David: The Tragedy of Errors," *New York Review of Books,* 9 August, 2001.

A realistic Middle East peace policy, however, could not be framed without facing up to the problem of Saddam Hussein.

A few days after Madrid, Colin Powell's diplomatic shuttle between Sharon and Arafat proved abortive; apparently neither man was willing to make the slightest concession, even though a week earlier the Israelis had withdrawn their troops from several Palestinian towns. This setback didn't mean that the trip would be entirely fruitless: over the long term, it laid the groundwork for future initiatives. Nevertheless, for the time being it had failed—a fact that the American press was the first to proclaim. But the farcical side of this tragic situation was the choir of European commentators who, from the loftiness of their intellectual and diplomatic sterility, sneered at the fiasco with their customary condescension.*

It would not be long before events prompted a reversal of the ridicule. On April 22, 2002, under increasing pressure from President Bush, Ariel Sharon's government resigned itself to lifting the siege of Arafat's headquarters in Ramallah that it had maintained since mid-December 2001. And Bush again insisted upon a complete and rapid evacuation of the Palestinian Territories by the Israeli army, in view of a new peace process he had outlined over several days with Crown Prince Abdullah of Saudi Arabia, whom he had invited to the United States. All this shows just how valid are the three pet assertions of European critics, namely:

1. Americans turn their backs completely on the Middle East.
2. When they do act, it is always what Israel wants.
3. Their initiatives are always failures.

Once again, facts could not silence the repetitive squawks of the anti-American parrots. On the occasion of the annual transatlantic summit that brought together the United States, the E.U. and Russia on May 2, 2002, the Washington reporter for TF1 television, Ulysse Gosset, on the *8 O'Clock News* compared President Bush's Middle East initiatives to the wavering shuffle of a tightrope walker who is about to take a tumble. Thus the "sheriff" cunningly deceives the gullible Europeans. One must

---

*With the happy exception, it must be added, of the French minister for foreign affairs, Hubert Védrine, who, in an opinion piece in *Le Monde* of 18 April 2002, made a balanced, intelligent and nuanced assessment of Powell's mission; he emphasized how difficult it really was and drew interesting lessons for future policy.

admire the subtlety of the vocabulary: sparing us the "cowboy," he serves us up the "sheriff." What artistry!

At that very moment, though, President Bush had just received assurance from the Israelis that they would raise the siege of Arafat's compound and proceed to withdraw a number of military units from Palestine. In addition—and not least among the breakthroughs—he had agreed in principle, and persuaded others to agree, to an international conference on the Middle East that, it was hoped, would begin in early summer. It would include the United States, the European Union and Russia. This was exactly what the nations involved had been angling for during the preceding months. (Incidentally, this decision alone is enough to refute the ritual accusation that America practices unilateralism exclusively.) Alongside this progress were intractable trouble spots, but these owed more to the Middle East's intrinsic problems than to any supposed American inertia. At any rate, America cut an activist figure compared with the European performance in this domain, as in many others.

The hostility that so often springs from an ambivalent fascination pushes too many Europeans to sink into the conviction that the United States is always at fault. But a government that is always wrong is just as mythical as a government that is never wrong. The American government makes mistakes sometimes, even frequently, as do all governments. When this happens, the American press and the U.S. Congress do not hold back in their reactions; in fact, their criticisms are usually more on target than what comes from abroad.

The hesitations of the Bush administration in the face of the Middle East crisis of 2001–2002, its zigzags that seemed to favor the Palestinians on one day and the Israelis on the next, then the perceptible disagreements among the top government officials—all these obstacles to an effective diplomacy were pointed out as mercilessly by Zbigniew Brzezinski (the distinguished historian and political analyst who had been Carter's national security advisor) as by the leading pundits.* In American dailies, the op-ed pages typically present opposing points of view and they are not labeled "Polemics"—which is customary in French newspapers, as if readers were not grownup enough to realize they are dealing with opinions and to form their own conclusions pro or con.

---

*See, for example, Fareed Zakaria, "Colin Powell's Humiliation," *Newsweek,* 29 April 2002.

Television debates as well, on the most varied themes in national politics and international affairs, regularly put into the ring competing advocates and experts who generally articulate radically opposing points of view with civility.

Because others criticize their policies and their society, Americans see it as their own duty to jump in first. And they often do this ferociously. But this is different from the knee-jerk automatism that too often propels Europeans into blanket condemnations of U.S. diplomacy as a permanent disaster and a harsh reflection on the whole American society.

■ ■ ■

ON THE APRIL 2002 first round of the presidential elections, France experienced the humiliation of seeing a demagogic populist of the extreme Right move ahead of the Socialist candidate, taking second place behind Jacques Chirac and thus going on to a runoff. What did Olivier Duhamel, professor at the Institute of Political Studies, Socialist deputy in the E.U. and one of our leading commentators, have to say about it? This pearl: "Now we are catching up with the degenerate democracies of the type of the United States, Austria and Italy."* In other words, it is we French who, with our votes, thrust Jean-Marie Le Pen to heights that he would never have been able to attain in a healthy democracy, but it is the American democracy that is degenerate. The results of the April 21 election were shameful, but we could take consolation in the belief that the Americans have been way ahead of us in this regard from time immemorial. Isn't America, after all, "structurally fascist"? The strange thing is that it is always in Europe that dictatorships and totalitarian regimes spring up, yet it is always America that is "fascist."

If Le Pen's share of the votes is combined with those won by the three Trotskyite candidates, the Communist Party and the Greens (who in France are leftist and Maoist more than environmentalist), one sees that one-third of the voters went for candidates from the extreme Left or the extreme Right who rejected what they called *mondialisation ultra-libérale,* which is to say economic liberty, mother of political freedom; evidently they wished to revert to a discredited protectionist *dirigisme* of an indisputably totalitarian flavor. Thus the charge of "degeneracy"

---

*Le Monde, 4 April 2002.

that the French, with their farcical airs of commiseration, lay on American democracy seems more truly applicable to their own. It would be nice if the French would learn to see themselves as they really are: saddled with an impractical and moribund constitution; with a government that is incapable of instilling respect for the law and knows how to say one thing only, "tax and spend"; with an intelligentsia that is ever blinder to the world and citizens who grow ever idler, convinced that they can always earn more while doing less.

Alas, the lessons to be learned from the embarrassment of the April 21 election were not taken to heart. Some commentators—among the most famous in French journalism—even blamed Jacques Chirac for Le Pen's rise: the outgoing president, by placing so much stress on security problems, had played into the hands of the National Front. It is strange to see professional journalists advising the suppression of information on the pretext that the truth might help the enemy. This old sophism evades acknowledging that if the truth is harmful to one's cause, it is because of the very facts that one hopes to suppress, or at least dodge responsibility for.

This applies to all French governments during the last two decades of the century insofar as questions of law and order are concerned. But instead of analyzing problems as they are in the here and now, the French have a compulsion to analogize them to events that happened long ago in contexts bearing no relation to the present. However good the (very different) reasons for criticizing Jörg Haider in Austria and Silvio Berlusconi in Italy, to compare their arrival on today's political scene to the Anschluss in 1938 on the one hand, and to the rise of Fascism in 1922 on the other, serves only to reveal a staggering historical ignorance. And the large numbers of demonstrators who took to the streets of French cities after April 21 to assail Le Pen by exhibiting swastikas had their calendars on the wrong year—they were reenacting prewar antifascist rituals. Fortunately the National Front does not have the means to indoctrinate and terrorize society that the National Socialists possessed. Each nation of the European Union is surrounded by solid democracy— so different from the Europe of the 1930s, riven by dictatorships. Rather than go shouting in the streets in imitation of seventy-year-old dramas, the "young" activists might have done better trying to understand the real origins and novel features of the National Front phenomenon. The demonstrators, whom Elizabeth Lévy cruelly but not groundlessly calls

157

"operetta antifascists," were putting on a show for themselves rather than engaging in a program befitting the circumstances.*

These reconstructed battles against yesterday's dangers explain the ineffectiveness of the battle that must be fought against today's perils. But the theatrics have a very specific function for the Left's defense mechanism—a fringe benefit, as it were, of its neurosis. Discredited by its complacent indulgence of, or complicity in, Communist genocides, the Left never stops imagining fascist dangers culled from the museums of history. According to its own version of history, the only real twentieth-century totalitarianism was Nazism, or more generally fascism in its multiple forms. Hence the incessant drumming on the subject of Hitler, the Holocaust, Mussolini and Vichy, whereas the chronicle of Communism's crimes, which have continued long after 1945, is always subject to vigilant censorship. Any book devoted to the topic sets off a counteroffensive against its author (or authors), on whom are dumped cartloads of mendacious calumnies, above all the accusation of serving the interests of Nazism and anti-Semitism. This practice is aimed at discrediting them, so as to avoid the duty of having to formulate replies.** But it is the Left whose loyalties we have to question.

It is not surprising if students, in their manifestos and demonstrations, call upon a truncated version of history: this is the expurgated version that prevails in secondary and university education. Jacques Marseille, himself an *hors caste* (pariah) historian, recounts: "When I sat on the examining board of the HEC,† I often questioned the students about Stalinism. Most of them replied with a straight face that Uncle Joe's mistake was to prioritize capital goods over the consumer goods sector. Then I would ask them if they weren't aware of any more serious transgressions—the Gulag, for example.... Amazing!"††

■ ■ ■

*Elisabeth Lévy, "L'antifascism ne passera pas," *Le Figaro,* 24 April 2002. And see the book by the same author, *Les Maîtres censeurs* (J. C. Lattès, 2002).

**For detailed descriptions of these tactics, I refer the reader to two of my own books: *La Grande Parade* (Plon, 2000; Pocket, 2001); and *La Nouvelle Censure* (Robert Laffont, 1977). In *La Grande Parade* I describe in particular the disgraceful defamatory treatment inflicted on the authors of *The Black Book of Communism.*

†*École des hautes études commerciales:* the top French business school, one of the *Grandes Écoles.*

††*Le Figaro,* 26 April 2002.

The fundamental role of anti-Americanism in this agenda will be readily understood. Europe in general and its Left in particular absolve themselves of their own moral failings and their grotesque intellectual errors
by heaping them onto the monster scapegoat, the United States of America. For stupidity and bloodshed to vanish from Europe, the U.S., contrary to every lesson of real history, must be identified as the singular
threat to democracy. Even during the Cold War, although it was the
U.S.S.R. that annexed Eastern Europe, made satellites out of several
African countries and invaded Afghanistan, and although it was the People's Republic of China that marched into Tibet, attacked South Korea
and subjugated three Indochinese countries, it remained dogma among
Europeans—from Sweden to Sicily, from Athens to Paris—that the only
power that could be fingered as "imperialistic" was America.

For somewhat different reasons than the Left, the European Right
widely shares this accusatory vision of America. In an April 2002 issue
of the conservative-leaning British weekly magazine the *Spectator,* Andrew
Alexander, a leader writer for the popular conservative newspaper the
Daily Mail, learnedly expounded the thesis that the Cold War was an
American plot. So, contrary to what some naïve witnesses (of whom I
was one) thought they saw, there never was a de facto annexation by
Moscow of most of Eastern Europe and the Balkans, no suppression of
the Prague Spring, no Berlin blockade, no insurrectionary strikes in
France and Italy—sinister warnings of Stalinist ambitions—and no Korean
War or civil war in Greece. How could we have been so credulous! All
those episodes, to the deep consternation of Stalin (who was well known
for his peaceful inclinations), were secretly fomented by the United States
as a pretext for planetary domination.

Following a similar logic, one might build a case that the Hundred
Years' War was a complete fabrication by Joan of Arc, who wanted star
billing in a pseudo-resistance against the conciliatory, peace-loving English.
Or that Czar Alexander I was responsible for the wild story that Napoleon
had led the Grande Armée into Holy Russia with the intention of
conquering her; with his claim to have routed the French, the czar was
seeking to justify in advance the subsequent occupation of Paris by his
own army. And didn't General de Gaulle, by the way, with Machiavellian
craftiness instill the nightmare of the German occupation into the minds
of the French, all so that he could use the imaginary catastrophe as a spring-
board for his 1944 accession to power? This style of topsy-turvy historical

revisionism will strike everyone as fantasmagoric and ludicrous, yet in the case of the United States it is deemed worthy of consideration and almost plausible. In *Le Monde* of April 25, 2002, Patrice de Beer, commenting on Andrew Alexander's lucubrations, avers that "his line of argument is convincing."* In contrast, recall that the argument of *The Black Book of Communism,* scholarly and accurate though it is, was judged unpersuasive.**

The European Right puts the United States on trial for good cause: that way it won't have to face up to its own blunders as a reason for America's emergence as a superpower. In the eyes of the Left, anti-Americanism has the added virtue of allowing it to wage its war on liberalism. *L'Humanité* of April 27, 2002, not in the least discouraged by the "final fall" of the Communist Party in the April 21 elections, wrote that the battle against the National Front is a battle against "fascism, racism and ultraliberalism." The theme never changes: it's a matter of associating liberalism with fascism. And the United States is, of course, the citadel of liberalism, and therefore of fascism. Let us note in passing that even when moribund, with its 3.4 percent of the vote, the Communist Party is so wedded to mendacity that it cannot keep from remaining faithful to the lie, even in its final breath. In fact, Le Pen is not at all liberal; he is antiliberal, not in spite but because of being an extreme rightist. He is just as anti-American as is the Left. Mussolini and Hitler were as violently hostile to liberalism as was Stalin, and for the same reason: they knew the intimate connection between liberalism and democracy. The principal object of their execration was the British democracy. For the totalitarians of today, whether called Laguiller or Le Pen, it is America that functions as the whipping boy.

Admittedly the Europeans, with intermittent bouts of common sense, often realize the futility of an obsessive anti-Americanism and can be the first to denounce its more extreme expressions. Commenting on the public opinion poll that I mentioned earlier, *Le Monde* enumerated some of them: "Puritan cretinism, barbarous arrogance, rampaging capitalism, hegemonic urges: these are the familiar themes that feed hatred for

---

*Sent as a special correspondent for *Le Monde* to Cambodia in 1975, Patrice de Beer distinguished himself for all time by eulogizing the Khmer Rouges when Phnom Penh was invaded by these notorious philanthropists.

**Stéphane Courtois et al., *The Black Book of Communism: Crimes, Terror, Repression,* ed. and trans. Mark Kramer, ed. Jonathan Murphy (Cambridge, Mass.: Harvard University Press, 1999).

America."* The charge of "puritan cretinism" was notably revived in Europe during the time of President Clinton's tribulations on account of his liaison with Monica Lewinsky. We Europeans and especially we French, as we kept repeating in the press and on the air, are far too sophisticated to meddle in the private lives of our officials and try to topple them from power when they happen to have an extramarital adventure. Besides the hypocrisy of the alleged American puritanism, Europeans invoked another misconception to explain the attack on Clinton: the Republicans were said to have orchestrated the campaign to impeach the president because they believed they held a sort of proprietary right to the White House and couldn't resign themselves to being displaced by a Democrat.

Like the majority of anti-American refrains, these two putative explanations rested on a charming disdain for easily verifiable facts. With regard to puritanism in general, it is well known that the movement for sexual liberation that spread in Europe at the close of the 1960s took off in America first. Women's gaining of the same sexual license as men, the coming-out of homosexuals from their closeted status, and other revolutions in mores came from the United States. If there was an American puritanism, it was the Americans who put an end to it, and in so doing they influenced Europe, which in turn moved forward in this area. As for the private lives of their leaders, they are just as respected in America as they are supposed to be in Europe. The whole world knew—or at least the journalists and the politicians knew—that Franklin D. Roosevelt had a mistress and that his wife, Eleanor, had a lover; but everyone was discreet about these. Likewise in the case of John F. Kennedy and his extravagant sex life. In reality, what Clinton was being blamed for was not his sexual adventure per se, but his bad taste in playing such a game in so public a space as the Oval Office, and above all his denying under oath the fact of his affair. For the president of the United States, guardian-in-chief of the Constitution, to commit perjury is incontestably grounds for impeachment.

To understand this, there is no need to imagine some Republican rancor over being dispossessed of the highest office in the land, an office of which they consider themselves the permanent occupants. Once more, this supposed long-term lease on the White House is a European myth

*Le Monde, 25–26 November 2001.

that generated the fantasy of a reactionary Republican plot against Clinton. Remembering some dates will demolish the myth. Not to rehearse the complete history of the American presidency, we will begin with Franklin Roosevelt's first term. A quick calculation shows that the Democrats occupied the White House from 1933 to 1953 (Roosevelt and Truman), from 1961 to 1969 (Kennedy and Johnson), from 1977 to 1981 (Carter), and finally from 1993 to 2001 (Clinton): in all, 40 years. Over the same period, the Republicans held the presidency from 1953 to 1961 (Eisenhower), from 1969 to 1977 (Nixon and Ford), and from 1981 to 1993 (Reagan and Bush père): in all, 28 years.

One really can't see what the alleged bitterness of the Republicans would be based on, seeing that they never had a monopoly on the White House that could have been stolen from them. So it isn't rocket science to see the nonsense of the allegations. But the willingness to see it apparently requires a superman.

■ ■ ■

Ideology is a mechanism for rejecting facts when they threaten to force a reexamination of cherished dogma. And it invents facts when necessary to the survival of dogma. In the domain of economic history, for example, it was indispensable to socialist ideologies to believe and to preach that the "ultraliberalism" of Ronald Reagan had impoverished the average American while further enriching the wealthy. Purportedly he had eliminated virtually all social protections, magnified inequalities, and reformed the tax system to the advantage of the most financially secure. This dogma once articulated, most commentators felt excused from any closer study of the economic history of the United States as it developed between 1980 and 2000.

Europeans could not be totally unaware of American economic growth during the last two decades of the century (interrupted by a brief recession in the early 1990s), nor of the rising standard of living that came with it and the tens of millions of new jobs that were created. But our imaginations remained fertile with ingenuous fantasies and denials designed to spare us the ordeal of facing up to the American success story and continental Europe's relative failure. For the first time since the end of World War II, Europe, so imbued with notions of its superiority, was again experiencing mass unemployment and the shame of a "new poverty" that made vagrants increasingly visible on the streets of our large cities. Our blindness and hypocrisy fed mainly on the myth that American growth profited only the wealthy and that the new jobs created were exclusively low-wage service jobs, whereas unemployment and marginalization in Europe were imbued with the benefits of our social justice and our "war against inequality."

A small effort of information-gathering would have sufficed to show the inanity of these evasions. The policies of the Republican Reagan, continued for the most part unaltered by the Democrat Clinton, reduced rather than exacerbated inequalities, particularly in the area of taxes. *The Economist,* in its issue of April 15, 2002, entitled an exhaustive study of Reagan's tax policies "The Age of Fiscal Socialism"*—evidently an ironic title, since the truths highlighted in the article painfully debunk the most cherished prejudices of continental Europeans. (I say "continental" because Great Britain under Margaret Thatcher escaped from these prejudices, and thus was held in the same opprobrium as Reagan's America, although Britain achieved an unemployment rate that was less than half of France's by the end of the 1980s.)

With his 1986 budget, President Reagan did indeed bring down the top marginal rate of federal income tax from 50 percent to 39.6 percent. But he also eliminated numerous exemptions and introduced a credit for low-income households. In effect, as Erik Izraelewicz comments, taxation on low incomes was reduced and taxation on the highest incomes was increased.** In 1979, those in the highest 20 percent income bracket gave the Internal Revenue Service, on average, 28.5 percent of their incomes; twenty years later, they gave 30 percent. At the other end of the scale, the income tax burden on the lowest quintile fell from 8.4 percent in 1979 to 4.6 percent today—an appreciable decrease. As for the middle class, the engine of consumption because it is the largest group, their burden of taxation returned to the level of 1966.

The famous economist Robert J. Samuelson, commenting on the Congressional Budget Office report of April 2002 that spelled out these statistics, observed that if the rich in America were indeed so powerful and had so much political clout, their tax burden would have gone down. Yet exactly the opposite had occurred, he noted, while government expenditures benefiting the middle class, the poor and seniors increased.

---

* *The Economist* draws from, among other sources, a report by the Congressional Budget Office published in April 2002.

**Erik Izraelewicz, "Reagan fut un vrai socialiste!" *Les Échos,* 5–6 May 2000. Izraelewicz is the editor in chief of *Les Échos,* a financial daily.

"Americans," concluded Samuelson, "live in a democracy. It is people who vote, not dollars. Our politicians tend to obey the will of the greatest number of voters, often at the expense of minorities."* (Samuelson, it is worth pointing out, is an editorial writer for the *Washington Post* and for *Newsweek,* both of which are considered to be left-leaning, or at least could not pass for cheerleaders of the Reagan administration.)

How is it that Europeans, except for some specialized publications and books with a limited readership, do not take these facts into consideration?

It could reasonably be argued that the vast majority of European citizens do not have the leisure to become experts in economics, and have other things to do than wade through CBO reports or even newspaper summaries. What about our politicians? Or the general run of our media? Their silence is all the more inexcusable in that one of the commonplaces of the anti-American vulgate is to accuse the American media of lacking curiosity about European affairs, and international affairs in general. The accusation is obviously groundless; but it should alert us to take extra care not to earn a similar accusation ourselves. I have used the expression "the general run of the media" because in Europe we have a financial press that is typically impartial and well informed, and on the airwaves, especially radio, we often hear highly competent economics analysts who are well aware of realities in America and elsewhere. Why does information that should be available to everyone, thanks to such commentators, seem to evaporate before touching our awareness and seldom penetrate the defenses of the large-circulation newspapers and primetime network news broadcasts?

European curiosity about events across the Atlantic is often lively, but also often highly selective. When the news about the American economy is bad, then all of a sudden the media's curiosity becomes frenzied and miraculously receptive to the latest data. On May 2, 2002, statistics published in Washington announced a rise in unemployment, which in April went from 5.2 percent to 6 percent—an increase the more incomprehensible, according to the Treasury Department, because GNP growth during the first trimester had reached the exceptionally high level of 5.5 percent per annum, while the European growth rate was stagnating at

---

*Robert J. Samuelson, "Think Again: Rich Special Interests Don't Rule in America," *International Herald Tribune,* 19 April 2000.

2 percent. Immediately the European media jumped greedily on this brief spiking of American unemployment. French radio and television, with each news update, gloated over this manna from heaven for two whole days following the initial revelation. They had been much less loquacious in the preceding year when U.S. unemployment remained at 4 percent—which economists consider equivalent to full employment—a figure that the French have not seen since the mid-1960s.

Imagine the shouts of triumph emanating from our government if, during the month of April 2002, French unemployment had fallen to 6 percent! But alas, it climbed from 9 percent to 9.3 percent (at the very least, for our numbers are always slightly embellished in the official beauty salons). Likewise, the international context of France's 2001 decline in unemployment, about which the Socialists were so boastful, went mostly unmentioned. Between 1998 and 2001, unemployment dropped throughout Europe thanks to a global economic recovery; in fact, France was one of the countries that saw the smallest declines in unemployment levels and therefore profited least from this recovery. With 9 percent unemployed (officially), we were far behind the United Kingdom (5.1 percent), Austria (3.9), Denmark (5.1), Sweden (4.0) and Switzerland (2.6). These comparisons, which relativize the vaunted Socialist success, were never drawn—at least I never heard them—on the mass media, who are so quick to sound the clarion when the American economy shows signs of faltering.

Many Europeans' image of America as the fortress of "ultraliberalism" is more than a mere oversimplification. As with many received ideas, it derives from a degree of ignorance, often carefully sustained by the so-called "information industry." In reality, the American government in many respects is going in the same direction as the European governments. It also is assailed by the innumerable pressure groups that aim to extort and generally succeed in getting subsidies, exemptions and protections of every kind—advantages that, as in Europe, will later prove to be irrevocable. When one mentions these lobbies, Europeans tend to imagine only the hand of "big Yankee capitalism."

But as we saw in Robert Samuelson's observation, the most powerful American lobbies are not the corporations; a much larger influence on the federal government is, for example, the American Association of Retired Persons (AARP), or the agricultural lobby (which is formidable in every developed country), or the American Federation of State, County and Municipal Employees (AFSCME), or the Hotel and Restaurant

Association, or hundreds of other groups representing millions of voters. According to a statistical study made in 1990 by the American Society of Association Executives—there *had* to be such an organization—at least seven out of ten Americans belong to an association of some kind, and a quarter of these claim membership in four or more. It has been a long time since "pressure group" and "lobby" ceased to designate only a handful of supposedly omnipotent capitalists.

"Today everyone is organized, and everyone is part of an interest group," writes Jonathan Rauch in a book whose title clearly states the author's thesis: *Government's End: Why Washington Stopped Working*.* In all the developed democracies, one sees this encircling of the state by special interest groups, some of which interfere with the government or with public services. As Rauch puts it, in a formula that recalls the lapidary style of Frédéric Bastiat, "[There are] two ways to become wealthier. One is to produce more. The other is to capture more of what others produce." The lobbies were created and multiplied precisely for the latter purpose: to perfect the art of profiting at the expense of fellow citizens while appealing to social solidarity and the common good. Indeed, sometimes a general interest is served, but rarely; most of the time, it's a matter of a parasitic sector grafted onto the productive economy. This is how a society is transformed bit by bit into a collection of special interests that stifle the government and inflate the tax burden. The United States hardly escapes, any more than other societies, this swaddling of the nation—contrary to what is imagined by European sages who believe the United States to be completely overrun by the "jungle" of "savage" and unbridled neoliberalism.

But Jonathan Rauch, in my opinion, is overly pessimistic when he characterizes the privileges extorted by particular interest groups as completely irreversible. It is true that in some nations, such as France, reform is virtually impossible because resistance to change is so deeply ingrained. But other nations are more capable of adaptation; their governments from time to time muster sufficient energy to loosen the corporatist shackles. We have seen this in Great Britain, Sweden, New Zealand and even Italy at the end of the last century. The United States, despite the crushing weight and ingenious efficiency of its lobbies, belongs to this group of countries that periodically achieve reforms allowing the public

*New York: Public Affairs, 1994.

to draw breath again—particularly by the lightening of some taxes or by the eradication of some wasteful public expenditures (which comes down to the same thing).

Paradoxically, judgmental Europeans are likely to excommunicate as "reactionaries" those American public officials who have the courage to attempt reforms. For example, Newt Gingrich, who became Speaker of the House when the Republicans gained the majority in the 1994 midterm elections, came in for this sort of treatment: in Europe he was bluntly depicted as a horrid right-winger, even a fascist. Why? Because, among other reasons, he wanted to reform the welfare system, something quite a few others had tried and failed to do. For a long time it had been proverbial, even among Democrats, that the welfare system was too costly, too inefficient and out of control. "The welfare mess" was a phrase commonly invoked in everyday political rhetoric for thirty years. Gingrich's intention was not to undermine justified social expenditures, but to end outright profligacy—though in America as elsewhere, it is such profligacy that best fattens the parasitic class. The goal, therefore, is to label wastefulness as "progressive." Hence the mass mustering of forces against reforms that would cut back excesses.

Another of Gingrich's projected reforms, one that ran aground, was the abolition or at least great reduction of agricultural subsidies. Here the French vociferations against "that awful little man" (a description that I heard on one of our major radio networks) were even more incomprehensible. It requires all the illogic that issues from blind hatred to rail continually against American agricultural subsidies and at the same time drag through the mud someone who aims precisely to reduce them.

In the history of European ideology, there has always been a hermetic, insurmountable and deeply rooted wall that divides the Left from the Right. In the United States, on the other hand, the parties may readily make common cause, as when congressional bills are jointly authored by a Democrat and a Republican, or when bills are passed on to an administration of the opposing party for implementation. It was Bill Clinton who, at the end of the day, ratified the North American Free Trade Agreement (NAFTA) between the U.S., Canada and Mexico—an accord negotiated by his Republican predecessor. And it was Clinton, interestingly enough, who pushed through welfare reforms initiated by the Reagan administration. Earlier, it was Richard Nixon who launched an environmental protection program at a time when the Left regarded this as a ploy to distract from the Vietnam War; and it was Nixon who promoted "affirmative action" for minorities.*

Whence arise the difficulties that Europeans have in understanding the process of reform and social progress in the United States? Since the beginning of the twentieth century, the terms of historical interpretation have been dictated by socialist ideology, and this tends to creep even into the thought of nonsocialists. The basic idea, to put it simply—but political notions for the most part *are* simple—is that class struggle is the sole motor of social progress. Capitalism can bring wealth only to a minority, while the ever-growing working masses, whom it steals from, are doomed to become ever poorer. Socialism's objective, then, can be nothing less than the abolition of capitalism, with the collective appropriation of the means of production and exchange, while liberalism's aim must be to prevent this appropriation by defending private property and enterprise. In parallel with the revolutionary socialism that advocated insurrection as the path to the dictatorship of the proletariat, there arose at the end of the nineteenth century a "reform" or "revisionist" socialism; but this differed only with respect to means, not the desired goal. Marxists in general, and not Communists alone, have always considered social democracy a betrayal of real socialism. In 1981, François Mitterrand berated Swedish Socialists for not having smitten capitalism with "a blow to the heart," and right at the end of the twentieth century the French Socialist Party severely castigated Tony Blair's "New Labour" agenda as a "degenerate" version of the true doctrine. In the first round of the French presidential election in 2002, nearly 25 percent of valid votes went to Trotskyite and pseudo-environmentalist candidates of the extreme Left; their hostility towards the market is shared by the protectionist extreme Right, which gave almost 17 percent of the vote to the National Front. Undoubtedly at least half of voters for the Socialist Party (roughly 8 percent nationally), in opposing free market globalization, are rejecting capitalism and economic liberty as such.

This conception of society as divided into two implacably opposed camps is foreign to American thinking. Early on, French analysts were asking themselves the question posed by the title of Werner Sombart's classic 1906 work, *Why Is There No Socialism in the United States?* The

---

*On these political realignments and compromises see Steven F. Hayward, *The Age of Reagan: The Fall of the Old Liberal Order* (Forum-Prima, 2002).

celebrated German sociologist answered that, first of all, universal suffrage was established in the United States as early as the beginning of the
nineteenth century. In contrast to contemporary Europe, from an early
date the American working class could participate in the political life of
the nation, actively taking part in associations and political parties—in
short, escaping the feeling of exclusion that, for the European proletariat,
accompanied the development of industrial society.

Sombart also argued that Americans avoided socialism because the
majority of the working class were immigrants from Europe. These people could compare what they had left behind against what they found
in the New World: a society that, despite economic and other forms of
inequality and often violent conflicts, was much less rigid than the Old
World's and much more conducive to upward mobility.* This is the social
mobility of the American Dream, so often derided by Europeans as a
myth, a snare and a delusion. Yet, as Pierre Weiss writes in his recent
introduction to Sombart, "The American worker likes to think of himself as—and in fact is—part of a socioeconomic system that assures him
a satisfying degree of participation." By the same token, since the beginning of the nineteenth century "his civic life makes him an active citizen."** The American Dream is not simply a matter of how to become
a millionaire; it has more to do with the osmosis between the working
and middle classes that was achieved much earlier and more extensively
than in Europe.

Already in 1906, Sombart saw in the economic, political and moral
condition of the American worker a foreshadowing of the European wage-
earner after 1950. For if America has never remotely been socialist in the
"revolutionary," Bolshevik sense of the term (the Communist Party has
always been microscopic and mainly composed of intellectuals and KGB
agents), it has, on the other hand, been undeniably social-democratic,
and on a vast scale. What was Roosevelt's New Deal if not a sweeping
social-democratic reform, perpetuated by Kennedy and Johnson, and
later under Republican presidents? In this respect Americans were ahead

---

*Since Sombart, social mobility has been the subject of numerous American studies;
among the best-known and most influential of these are Seymour Martin Lipset's, in
particular his *Social Mobility in Industrial Society* (University of California Press,
1959).

**From a recent French translation by Pierre Weiss, with an introduction by him
(PUF, 1992).

of Europe, where—after World War II and especially between 1980 and 2000—the various socialist parties, haphazardly and piecemeal, gave up on revolutionary rhetoric; one after the other they were won over to social democracy, catching up with New Deal reformism.

Thus collapses one of the chief accusations of the European Left against the United States. This one revolved around the notion that the "American Left"—a term of abuse dripping with implied scorn for our own French *"social-traîtres"*—was not authentically of the Left; after all, it was content with some cautious retouching of the system, rather than a complete transformation.* Looking back over the past two centuries, American society has, in the long term, experienced a far more precocious, realistic and continuous dynamic of change than have European societies, where spasmodic upheavals, revolutionary only in appearance, more often than not have resulted in setbacks. In the political, economic, social and even cultural realms, our condescending arrogance and conformism tell us more about our own weaknesses than about the alleged deficiencies of the Americans.

Here we see how the Americans are useful to us: to console us for our own failures, serving the myth that they do worse than we do, and that what goes badly with us is their fault. America is the scapegoat, made to bear all the sins of the world.

---

*On this subject, see Seymour Martin Lipset's "L'Américanisation de la gauche européenne" in *Commentaire,* Autumn 2001.

Conclusion

THE ANTI-AMERICAN OBSESSION, in effect, aggravates the evil that it aims to extirpate, namely the unilateralism famously ascribed to the United States. By criticizing the Americans whatever they do, and on every occasion—even when they are in the right—we Europeans (and we are not alone in this, although we lead the dance) compel them to disregard our objections—even when *we* are in the right. The American reflex, conditioned by the constant avalanche of anathemas coming at them, causes them to keep thinking: "They're always blaming us, so why consult them at all? We already know they'll only vilify us."

An example: the increase in American agricultural subsidies in spring 2002. This undoubtedly deserved censure, though coming from the Europeans it was more than a little suspect, in view of two well-known facts. The first is that the European Union, through the Common Agricultural Policy (CAP), supports its farmers to the tune of four times per annum what American farmers receive in subsidies. Agricultural subsidies are the biggest item in the E.U. budget. Europeans, and above all the French, are not in a good position to reproach other countries for subsidizing their farmers, however objectionable this choke on the free market may be. The second reason is that in the age of international markets we have heard demonstrators, intellectuals, union bosses and governments around the world denounce the deregulation of trade as a disaster, especially for the poorest—causing unemployment, enslaving workers to profiteering capitalism, and at the end of the day subordinating the world economy to that of the United States.

So if Europeans see in liberalism only a mask for the forward march of American unilateralism, they should not oppose at least a corrective dose

171

of protectionism. Why, then, are they so quick to blame protectionism with as much virulence as they do liberalism, as long as both are practiced by the United States? An American can draw but one conclusion: It isn't liberalism or protectionism that Europeans find loathsome; it is America.

The American protectionist move came under fire from European commissioner Franz Fischler; after announcing his opportune and well-justified intent to put the United States on the dock with the World Trade Organization, he added: "But the French shouldn't be complacent. It won't profit us to keep the Common Agricultural Policy too extravagant."* And it's true that the French are always opposing CAP reform. The lesson to draw from this is that if the United States does have a tendency towards unilateralism, it can only be reinforced by such an imbroglio. The U.S. hears European governments constantly upbraiding her with reproofs that are never directed against themselves and, what's more, that are pathetically self-contradictory. It's no wonder if she might prefer to act alone.

If the anti-American obsession leads to self-contradiction even when the United States has a bad track record, it becomes even more intellectually confused when the record can be defended. An example: throughout 2001, China, Russia and the European Union attacked George W. Bush for putting the antimissile defense program (Strategic Defense Initiative) back on the agenda. The polemic had actually preceded the Bush administration. In 1999, when the U.S. Congress, on a bipartisan vote, had mandated President Clinton to reinstate research on antiballistic missiles, the reaction was sharply critical even in the United States, where the "Star Wars" program had always had determined foes, beginning with the *New York Times.* Then in France: Hubert Védrine, the socialist foreign minister under Prime Minister Jospin, wrote to Secretary of State Madeleine Albright to express his government's concern over the "destabilizing effect" of an ABM system. President of the Republic Jacques Chirac, although politically opposed to Jospin, jumped onto the bandwagon, announcing—in "full agreement" with the presidents of Russia and China—that the American project threatened to "revive the arms race."

This furious assault on the antimissile shield recycled arguments left over from the Reagan presidency, when the SDI was first proposed. These arguments boil down to two main ideas:

Figaro Économie, 14 May 2002.

1. An antiballistic missile defense system is unworkable. It is a charade, a Pentagon propaganda scheme. It is a "fraud," a minister in the Jospin government told me; it's a "bluff," averred another highly placed official.

2. Such a system represents a threat to nuclear parity between the superpowers as defined in the 1972 ABM treaty. It would destroy the whole balance-of-power edifice that guarantees international security.

It hardly takes a superhuman mental effort to see how incompatible these two propositions are. Either the antimissile system is a derisory mystification doomed to be forever ineffective, or it will enable the United States to neutralize the nuclear capability of the other powers and thus incite another arms race. (But the first proposition, surely, is a matter to be determined empirically.)

Those who make these mutually exclusive assertions show a degree of irresponsibility that should disqualify them from the geopolitical debate. They also refuse to take account of the fundamental changes that have transformed the international strategic game in the closing years of the century. The ABM treaty was based on the doctrine of "mutually assured destruction" (MAD), which of course was a product of the Cold War. By now, this doctrine is entirely out of date. The threat of a preemptive missile strike by Russia against the United States, or vice versa, has simply disappeared, and the treaties designed to stave off such an eventuality are obsolete. On the other hand, new dangers have emerged: dictatorships that have acquired and continue to accumulate chemical, biological and even nuclear arsenals. These rogue states have no respect for treaties and they permit no monitoring. International terrorism, in its vast scope and highly organized nature, is another unprecedented danger calling for unprecedented retaliatory measures.

Europeans' voluntary blindness with regard to these radical changes renders any American attempts at dialogue fruitless; as a result, America has no other option but to make unilateral decisions. How can you discuss a problem with people who deny its very existence? What must the president of the United States have thought when, on an official visit to Berlin at the end of May 2002, he saw thousands of demonstrators holding aloft placards with the slogan "NO TO WAR"? How could so many thousands of Europeans have the effrontery to announce so clearly that they viewed the war in Afghanistan as a case of American aggression? And how could they clamor—not only against the United States but against their own interests, and against the interests of democracy and the liberation of oppressed peoples everywhere—that whatever Saddam Hussein had done, no attempt must be made to rid the world of him? The European Left has clearly learned little from the history of the twentieth century. It remains fanatically opposed to moderates, and moderate towards fanatics.

Then on May 26, 2002, demonstrators paraded against the presence of George W. Bush when he went on to visit Paris. Again, America was vilified for its "warmongering and drive for domination," purportedly the sole motive for its intervention in Afghanistan. Here the protestors' sectarianism and incivility were matched only by the cynicism with which they evaded the reality of Islamic hyperterrorism.

This reversal of culpability has eloquent advocates. Three days after September 11, the well-known Brazilian economist Fidel Furtado published an article in one of his nation's most important periodicals setting forth his theory of the disaster: that the destruction of the World Trade Center was a plot engineered by the American extreme Right so as to create a situation opportune for seizing power. This great Brazilian intellectual compares 9/11 to the Reichstag fire of 1933, allegedly set by the Nazis so they could blame the Left and have a pretext to suspend constitutional protection of personal rights, the beginning of the totalitarian regime. No matter that this sort of putsch has never been a factor in American history, whereas in Brazil . . . no more need be said. But always the imperative is to project our faults onto America so as to absolve ourselves. Another Brazilian, the theologian Leonardo Boff, wrote in the daily newspaper *O Globo* that he regretted that only one plane had crashed into the Pentagon: much better if there had been twenty-five.* A fine display of Christian charity indeed. These cynical assessments and vindictive wishes were advanced in a nation that has nothing to do with Islam, where no mullahs preach a hysterical version of the Qur'an or hawk holy war to fanaticized mobs.

In these circumstances, one can understand why, on July 1, 2002, the United States withdrew from the International Court of Justice, whose 1998 founding treaty was signed in Rome. A good many friends of the United States deplored this decision. But given the blatant lies, the ridiculous fictions, the imaginary accusations that every day misrepresent Amer-

---

O Globo, 11 November 2001.

ican policies, it was foreseeable that thousands of prosecutors all over the world might summon before the court the entire executive branch of the U.S. government along with various members of Congress on charges of crimes against humanity. The impartial functioning of such a sensitive body as an international tribunal requires a minimum of good faith among all the signatory nations. America is justified in thinking that good faith towards her is not what prevails nowadays.

The "good faith" in question is displayed in commentaries on details of American social policy as well as major diplomatic and strategic developments.

An example of the former: on May 8, 2001, the U.S. Department of Education announced that henceforth, public schools would not have to be coeducational; coeducation had been the rule since 1972, when Congress prohibited single-sex schools. The reason for this change was the finding that in private education, where coeducation was not mandatory, single-sex schools delivered better results for both boys and girls; as a result, parents had been taking their children out of state-run schools and sending them to private institutions. So, hoping to improve public school performance, the DOE allowed public schools the freedom to go single-sex if they so wished. But the European press wouldn't buy this explanation. The real reason, they charged, had nothing to do with educational standards: it was really a reactionary maneuver emanating from George W. Bush and his cronies, who wanted to cater to the Christian Right's concern for their children's chastity. To realize just how absurd this theory is, it should be enough to point out that the new directive was backed by one of the most militant feminists in the United States: none other than the Democrat senator for New York, Hillary Rodham Clinton.

With respect to diplomacy and strategy, the case against U.S. "unilateralism" ought to have been dropped—at least provisionally—when President Bush made the rounds of the European capitals to consult with his allies. And the accusation that he was disinclined to accept arms reductions likewise ought to have been attenuated when, on May 24 in Moscow, the United States signed an agreement with Russia whereby each party undertook to reduce its nuclear arsenal to a number between 1,700 and 2,200 warheads by 2010, down from somewhere between 6,000 and 7,300 deployed by both sides in 2002. But again the European officials, commentators and journalists sulked, declaring that the two American initiatives proved neither a willingness to dialogue nor a renunciation

of the arms race. Bush, they said, remained obsessed with his antiterrorist "crusade" and prey to imaginary fears—the fanciful nature of which
the Europeans had no doubt just verified, since terrorists had recently
slaughtered dozens of German and French people in Tunisia and Pakistan. To lay blame on the Americans at every turn, whatever they do
and whatever happens to us, allows our elites to write off our dead as an
acceptable loss. If Bush keeps insisting on the terrorist threat, that proves
the danger doesn't exist and our fellow countrymen haven't been massa-
cred—or maybe just a few of them.

It remains essential—and this is a point I have made time and time
again in this book—that the superpower's excesses, actual or potential,
should be subject to our vigilant criticism; also, that we should insist on
our right to participate in those decisions of the superpower that affect
everyone. But this vigilance and this insistence haven't the slightest chance
of being taken seriously by the United States if our criticisms and demands
are not pertinent and rational.*

The often extravagant ravings of anti-American hatred, the media
imputations—sometimes the product of incompetence, sometimes of
mythomania—the opinionated ill will that puts the United States in an
unfavorable light at every turn, can only confirm for Americans the use-
lessness of consultation. The result is the exact opposite of what is sought.
The fallacies of the anti-American bias encourage American unilateralism. The tendentious blindness and systematic hostility of most of the
governments that deal with America can only lead to their own weakening, a progressive distancing from reality. And so America's confused enemies and allies alike, valuing animosity over influence, condemn themselves
to impotence—and thus, in effect, strengthen the country they claim to
fear.

---

*Take, for example, the speech made by George W. Bush on June 24, 2002, on the
subject of the Middle East. The president was blamed for wanting to remove Arafat
and "impose" other leaders on the Palestinians. But he made no mention of imposing anyone; rather, he spoke of working towards elections, hoping that "the Palestinian people elect a new leadership that is not compromised by [its participation in]
terrorism." What is unreasonable about such a hope? Especially when, in the same
speech, Bush said that once a real Palestinian state had been established, the Israelis
should return to the 1967 frontiers and accept the existence of a Palestinian zone in
Jerusalem—which amounts to a total rejection of Sharon's intent.